T3-BGM-039

FarEasternEconomic
REVIEW

VIETNAM
NOTEBOOK

By Murray Hiebert

Hanoi Correspondent — *Far Eastern Economic Review*

Published in Hongkong by Review Publishing Company Limited
G.P.O. Box 160, Hongkong
© Review Publishing Company Limited 1993
ISBN 9-627-01052-9

Contents

CHINA

Ha
Giang

Lai Chau
Lao
Cai
Cao
Bang

Dien
Bien Phu

Vinh
Yen

HANOI
Haiphong
Nam Dinh

LAOS

Thanh Hoa

Vinh

Gulf of
Tonkin

Hainan Is.

VIETNAM

Quang Tri
Hue

South China
Sea

Da Nang

THAILAND

Quang
Ngai

Kontum
Pleiku

Qui Nhon

CAMBODIA

Ban Me
Thout

Nha Trang

Da Lat
Cam Ranh

Mekong

Phan Thiet

Gulf of
Thailand

Ho Chi
Minh City

Roads
Railways

Vinh Loi

km
0   200

4

Foreword

By Nayan Chanda
Deputy Editor, *Far Eastern Economic Review*

Vietnam, a thin sliver of land jutting from China's underbelly to the South China Sea, was an unlikely candidate to be the "Middle Kingdom." But thanks to an epochal war involving the world's biggest superpower, it became one for the media.

For over a decade, the Vietnam War held the centre stage of world attention. However, once the dramatic images of tanks crashing through Saigon's presidential palace faded from the television screens, Vietnam was promptly returned to obscurity. It returned fleetingly to world view when tens of thousands of Vietnamese boat people took to the sea, looking for new homes, and when the Vietnamese crossed swords with their former allies, China and the Khmer Rouge in Cambodia.

However, with the Cold War over and the Soviet Union turned into a bad memory, things have begun to change — even in parts of Asia where time seems to hang heavy. One of the most noticeable developments has been the stirrings of change in Vietnam. Vietnam's communist revolutionaries, who defeated the Japanese and the French, and won the war against the Americans, have been forced to go back to school.

This time it is not to learn the art of war but economics and management. Faced with the loss of economic and military aid from Moscow, continuing international isolation brought by the US trade embargo, and the threat of losing its mandate from an increasingly disgruntled population, Vietnam has embraced reforms. By dismantling rigid central planning, encouraging private enterprise and opening the country to foreign investment, the Vietnamese have taken the first steps towards a far-reaching transformation.

More striking than selective liberalisation attempted from the top has been the dramatic changes sweeping every aspect of Vietnamese life. From writers publishing the country's first antiwar, even anticommunist, novels to entrepreneurs setting up pyramid schemes, from monks agitating for more freedom to *mama sans* plotting with the police to operate high-class brothels — Vietnam has been a place of fast-moving changes. This volume offers fascinating glimpses of a new Vietnam from the inside.

While hundreds of reporters and television crew roamed Vietnam during the war, precious few have followed, much less chronicled, the remarkable changes taking place in the post-war Vietnam of *doi moi*, or transformation.

The *Far Eastern Economic Review* was the first international news magazine to open a bureau in Hanoi in 1990. The Review has been fortunate to have as talented a reporter as Murray Hiebert as its first correspondent in Hanoi. A long-time student of Vietnam, conversant in the language, Murray has offered *Review* readers a unique perspective on the transformation. He has travelled through all walks of life in the new Vietnam, from Hanoi's halls of power to the lowliest factory floor, from military barracks to dissident intellectual's living room, and has provided us a fascinating montage of an old civilisation in the twilight of a new dawn.

This selection of his articles, deftly edited by John Leger, should prove a marvellous introduction to a country poised to emerge as a new Asian Tiger.

One Nation — or Two?

The north rules, but the south runs

HANOI — Northern Vietnamese writer Nguyen Manh Tuan could not wait to go to the south after communist tanks crashed into the gates of the presidential palace in Saigon in April 1975, toppling the government and ending more than a century of almost uninterrupted division of Vietnam.

In 1963, as the war was escalating, zealous communist rulers had sent Tuan, the son of a former capitalist book publisher in Hanoi, to the countryside as a "youth volunteer," building roads and cutting trees. When he was finally freed 12 years later, Tuan was bitter and wanted to get as far from the north as possible.

"At that time, I didn't think about whether the south was better than the north," the 47-year-old best-selling novelist recalls. "I just wanted to find a new life."

What he found fit many of the popular conceptions about the differences between north and south Vietnam. "In the initial days after liberation, the south enjoyed a more liberal atmosphere," he says. "Many novels not allowed in the north could be published here." That is because provincial departments of ideology and culture have considerable leeway in deciding what books local publishing houses can print.

But Tuan, whose popular novels often criticise the abuses of the Communist Party, is quick to point out that these differences have not remained static. "In the past four or five years, the north has become more liberal than the south," he argues. "Some of my recent novels which had been banned in the south have been published in the north."

Tuan's early experiences in Ho Chi Minh City, formerly known as Saigon, fit the stereotypes of most Vietnamese and foreigners about the differences between north and south Vietnam. Because of the history of foreign involvement in the south and the easier living conditions there, important — albeit often exaggerated — social, psychological, political and economic differences have emerged between the two halves of the country.

Many observers see significant personality differences, viewing southerners as more open-minded and adventurous. "Northerners are upright, traditional and conservative," argues an overseas Vietnamese businessman working in Ho Chi Minh City. "Southerners are easygoing and loud-mouthed. Northerners are like the British, while southerners are like Australians."

Southerners are often more direct in their speech. "When I go to a conference, northerners talk about problems in a roundabout way and avoid controversial points," says Tran Bach Dang, a southern intellectual who headed the Communist Party in Saigon during the war. "In the South, we like to be outspoken and direct, regardless of whether we're right or wrong."

Northerners also are more thrifty and never tire of telling tales about a mythological prince from the far south who lit his cigarettes with paper money. Many northern parents urge their children not to marry southerners because they have a reputation for wasting money.

Much of this attitude towards money is determined by environmental differences. The north is regularly ravaged by typhoons and has a wet, bitterly cold winter, while the south is blessed with a more moderate tropical climate. In addition, the north is much more densely populated, causing serious land shortages and forcing northerners to work much harder.

Population pressures had forced Vietnamese peasants a millennium ago to begin leaving the Red River delta — the 4,000-year home of their ancestors — and move south. By the 15th century, they had pushed south to what is now central Vietnam and had conquered the Cham empire. Two centuries later they had arrived in the Mekong delta and began pushing out the Khmer, or Cambodians.

Many of those who moved south were poor people without land, renegades, political exiles or criminals, much like the first Europeans who migrated to Australia. "As they moved south, they left behind much of their heritage," says archaeologist-historian Tran Quoc Vuong. "The influence of Confucianism and China weakened," he says, referring to the nearly 1,000-year Chinese occupation of Vietnam.

Vuong and others argue that the southern migrants assimilated numerous language and cultural traits from the Cham and the Khmer, who in turn had been influenced by Indian culture, including Brahmanism. The Cham and the Khmer also affected the world-view of the arriving Vietnamese.

"Hanoi had no seaport; it was the capital of the peasantry," Vuong says. "The Cham and the Khmer were open to the sea, so the new arrivals became more open-minded." He adds: "The march south brought people much closer to Southeast Asia. In the north, people always have one eye looking back" at their northern neighbour: China.

These regional differences were accentuated in the last half of the 19th century with the arrival of the French colonial rulers, who divided the country into north, south and central Vietnam. The South was colonised outright, while the other two parts were ruled as protectorates.

The French introduced Napoleonic law in the south, while the legal system in the other two regions was a hybrid, continuing to use many laws drawn up by the Vietnamese emperors. Ironically, because there was more freedom to speak and publish in Saigon, many northern revolutionaries moved south to launch their struggle against France.

After the defeat of the French in 1954, Vietnam became the focus of the cold war struggle between communism and capitalism. The north lived under an austere Stalinist regime, while the south was heavily influenced by the West, especially the US.

Although the formal division of Vietnam continued, the next two decades of war brought about large-scale movements of people. Millions of northerners went south either to flee communism or as soldiers to fight for national reunification, while hundreds of thousands of southern revolutionaries regrouped to the north.

Wide-scale migration, particularly from the north to the south, has continued since the end of the war. In the late 1970s, tens of thousands of northerners headed south either to help enforce Hanoi's control or to be reunited with their families. Others came seeking economic opportunity.

While the large influx of northerners helped to break down regional barriers, it also exacerbated long-standing north-south animosities. A good number of northerners came south with instincts of the victorious and the vanquished, says a foreign businessman who has long worked in Vietnam.

Many southerners were unhappy at the economic transformation programme imposed by Hanoi in 1978, which caused the economy to nosedive. Southerners often call people from the north "Bac Ky," a pejorative term dating to the French period, to remind them that they are different. Of course, many northerners have been fully integrated in the south, but they are often referred to as "honorary southerners."

"National concord has been a problem since reunification," observes a southern journalist. "Seventeen years is not enough to forget and normalise relations."

Few Vietnamese believe these frictions will result in renewed regional conflict, but some observers think Hanoi could face political turmoil in the south in the future. "The south's living standard is higher, so their demand for democracy is greater," says an official from the south working in the north. "If Hanoi puts too much pressure on the south, maybe people will resist."

The south, whose infrastructure is often described as 30 years ahead of that in the north, thanks to American aid during the war, is the engine driving Vietnam's economic development, producing more than half of the country's gross domestic product with less than a third of its population.

The per-capita income of Ho Chi Minh City is estimated at US$480, more than twice the national average of less than US$200. The city provides 40% to 60% of the entire national budget and helps to subsidise poorer provinces.

If the Mekong delta, Ho Chi Minh City's hinterland, is added to the equation, the figures become even more star-tling. This area, which accounts for 25% of the country's population, produces 48% of Vietnam's rice and all of its grain exports. In addition, all of Vietnam's 27 million barrels of oil exports and 60% of its seafood exports in 1991 origi-nated in the south.

"It is easy for southerners to adapt to a free-market economy," says Dang, the southern intellectual. "They were born in a capitalist atmosphere. It's more difficult for north-erners who suffered in agricultural cooperatives for 30 years."

Many of the economic reforms introduced nationwide in recent years were tried in the south first. Ho Chi Minh City was the first to introduce piece-work salaries in the late 1970s in an effort to boost sluggish production. It also experimented first with the one-price system, which effectively ended costly subsidies for commodities such as rice.

Deputy Mayor Pham Chanh Truc points out that Ho Chi Minh City never fully implemented Hanoi's "socialist trans-formation" scheme and allowed many small private produc-ers to continue operating after 1978. It also gave "big capital-ists" the right to resume production in 1985, more than a year before the measure was approved by the party's sixth congress, he says.

Other reforms came from the fertile Mekong delta provinces. An Giang province, bordering Cambodia, distributed land to farm families a full year before the move was approved by the party Politburo in 1988. Provincial officials also began closing money-losing state enterprises two years before Hanoi authorised the move. Today only 27 of An Giang's 150 state companies remain.

Much of the impetus for Vietnam's economic reforms has come from southern leaders, particularly Nguyen Van Linh and Vo Van Kiet, who led Ho Chi Minh City in the late 1970s and early 1980s before they were called to Hanoi. Linh, who was born in the north but spent most of his adult life in the south, mounted the current reform programme as party chief from 1986-91. Premier Kiet was born in the Mekong delta, and his heir apparent — Phan Van Khai — also hails from the south.

Although the party in the south has been willing to experiment with the economy, many southerners complain that it is politically more conservative than its counterpart in the north. "The economic reforms and new discos give the feeling of big change in Ho Chi Minh City," one intellectual observes. "But in political life, there have been no important changes for the past 15 years. Maybe they think they must hold the city more secure politically when they open the economy."

There are also significant religious differences between the north and the south. The north is mainly Confucian and Buddhist, and has witnessed a sharp revival of traditional folk festivals — commemorating local heroes, gods or goddesses — since the party launched its reforms.

In the south, no similar folk festivals have developed and the influence of Confucianism is weaker. At the same time, several indigenous, eclectic religious sects have taken hold in the south, which have frequently clashed with both the US-backed and communist regimes.

The north has more Buddhist pagodas, but the south has more monks. Some observers argue that southerners are more strict in following Buddhist principles, pointing out that they follow a vegetarian diet four days each month while most northerners do not.

But some southern Buddhists are also more politically active than their northern counterparts. Monks in the south captured world attention by immolating themselves to protest abuses by the US-backed regime during the war. Several prominent southern monks from Ho Chi Minh City's An Quang Pagoda are under house arrest for clashing with the new communist authorities, while northern monks have been more willing to cooperate with the party.

Catholic services in the north have changed little since the beginning of the century, and men and women still sit on opposite sides of the cathedral. In the south, church services are modern, women and men sit together and many priests play active social roles.

Although economic life is more buoyant in the south, most Vietnamese agree that intellectual life is more vibrant in the north. Many observers attribute this to the north's long mandarin-scholar tradition. For example, the north had 1,000 such scholars in the 1820s, while the south had only one.

Dang, the southern intellectual, adds that the different pace of life in the north also contributes to the different intellectual style. "Southern intellectuals only talk about things which are close to their daily life and the economic situation. They don't talk about questions of freedom, political pluralism or a multi-party system," he argues. "But in the north the economy is still at a standstill, so they have time to drink tea and talk about the major issues affecting Vietnam."

But some southerners say the difference is also because Hanoi grants greater intellectual freedom to northerners. A southern journalist points out that the majority of intellectuals in the north are "Communist Party members or have lived under communism for a long time, so the party gives them the right to criticise. If I talked like that, they'd say I was trying to work against the communist regime."

He has a point. Duong Thu Huong, a Hanoi writer arrested for attacking the party and calling for greater political openness, was released after six months. But in Ho Chi Minh

City, Nguyen Dan Que, a doctor and Vietnam's first member of Amnesty International, was sentenced to 20 years for roughly the same thing.

Newspapers are also different. Several Ho Chi Minh City newspapers have begun publishing in colour and regularly print articles sharply criticising government policies and high-level officials. Most Hanoi publications are still dull and cautious.

The style and content of writers also differ between north and south. "There are very few good writers in the south," argues a northern literary expert, pointing out that the north

is better known for its poetry and colourful language. "Southern novels are mainly romantic love stories. They don't have deep social analysis like in the north."

Tuan, the writer who migrated south, attributes this difference to economics. "Northern writers think southern writers consider money as their god," he complains. "The problem is that in the south we have to write to live. Writers in the north can still survive with state subsidies."

Writer Nguyen Manh Tuan.

Musicians describe similar differences. "Northern audiences appreciate us more," say the rock-singing couple, The Hien and Ha Lan, who were born in 1954. "Southerners have the chance to hear many more musical performances."

They say northern musicians have more trouble being accepted in the south than southerners have in the north. "When a good northern singer comes south he only gets small audiences," Ha Lan says. "Southerners love pop music but northern voices are only suitable for classical music."

Savers vs Spenders

Different lifestyles are linked to the climate

HAI HUNG — Seen from the air, the major river deltas of Vietnam look only slightly different. But at ground level, they are a world apart. A visit to Hai Hung and An Giang provinces — separated by nearly 2,000 kilometres — drives home the differences that history, geography and climate have produced between north and south Vietnam.

The lush green of the Mekong delta in the south is dotted with dwellings in a haphazard fashion, while the fields in the northern Red River delta look more organised, with dykes and canals and houses grouped in clusters that are often surrounded by a bamboo hedge. On closer look, one sees more tile-roofed brick houses in the Red River delta than in the south, where houses are often just made of wood or thatch.

Dat, a 48-year-old farmer in Tien Vy village in the Red River delta province of Hai Hung, welcomes visitors with the same cup of tea as his fellow farmer, Quang, in the south. But Dat serves tea inside a brick house with new furniture, a big cassette player and a Japanese television set.

Quang receives his guest on the porch of his simple, two-room wooden house. Although he produced three times as much rice as Dat in 1991, Quang has not purchased a motorbike or television set.

Since the Communist Party returned land to the tillers in 1989, Dat the northern farmer has managed to build a brick house for his family and a second one for his oldest son. He even had money left over to buy a motorcycle (from former

East Germany) and contribute to the reconstruction of the local 300-year-old Buddhist pagoda, which had fallen into disrepair before the party abandoned its march towards socialism in 1986. In late 1992, he planned to build another house for his second oldest son, who is getting married.

Dat, who has five children, says his income from rice production has doubled since the village cooperative gave him nearly two hectares of land in 1988. "Now I work on the land less than when I was part of the cooperative," he says, "but I produce more because I use more fertiliser and tend my plants more carefully."

Despite the efforts of Dat and those of his three children who still live at home, most of their income does not come from rice production. "Our village has too little farm land and two many labourers," complains the former soldier, who fought against the Americans in the south during the late 1960s.

Because of unusually cold weather in the spring of 1991, Dat produced only 8.5 tonnes of rice in two crops that year. He used some of this to feed his family and fed the rest to his pigs, which provide his most important source of income.

Hanoi's reforms have had a radically different impact on Quang, a once-wealthy 56-year-old Mekong delta peasant in Vinh Hung Hoi village in An Giang province, not far from the Cambodian border. He had farmed 10 hectares of his own land and rented an additional 20 hectares before the communists confiscated it in the late 1970s. In 1989 they told him he could have his land back, if he compensated the farmers currently using it.

Quang says this was difficult because after he lost his land, he spent all of his savings and had even been forced to sell his Japanese hand tiller, motorbike and television set to support his 10 children. As a result, he could afford to buy back only five hectares of land, which had belonged to his family for four generations. It cost him 25 tonnes of rice.

In 1991, Quang's plot produced 24 tonnes of rice, an amount that Dat in the north can only imagine in his wildest dreams. An Giang province in 1991 produced 829 kilogrammes of rice per person, nearly three times Hai Hung's 297 kilogrammes.

In addition, the size of Quang's field is too large for him and the three children remaining at home to handle, so they have begun hiring as many as 10 landless peasants to help them plant and harvest their rice. The use of hired farm help is still almost unheard of in the north.

Not only has this been anathema to the north's communists for nearly four decades but, even in relatively well-off northern provinces such as Hai Hung, farmers like Dat do not have enough land even to provide full-time work for their children. Hai Hung has only 128 square metres of farmland per person, roughly half of An Giang's 220 square metres.

Although Quang's neighbours consider him rich, he has not built a new house or bought a new motorbike or television set. He thinks it will be "10-20 years before I can afford to buy a new hand tiller."

The different climate of north and south Vietnam has had a major impact on how peasants spend their money. A peasant in the north builds a brick house as soon as he can afford it to protect himself against the harsh winters and frequent typhoons and floods. In the south, which has a more moderate tropical climate, even wealthy farmers are content with wooden or thatch houses. Many northern peasants have built cement or brick courtyards for drying their rice, while southerners dry their crops on the side of the road.

"Farmers in the north need to save because they will be hit by typhoons, floods and cold weather," says Nguyen Khac Vien, a retired French-trained medical doctor who founded Hanoi's first child-psychology research centre. "In the south, it's easy to grow rice or catch fish so farmers don't have to save money."

"If a northern farmer catches a fish or raises a chicken, he takes it to the market to sell," Vien adds. "If a southerner catches a fish or raises a chicken, he buys a bottle of wine and invites his friends over for a feast."

Quang insists he is still poor, even though his neighbours

consider him rich. He points out that buying his old land back cost him a lot. Moreover, he insists he made no money in 1991 from his 24-tonne harvest because it sold for only Dong 700-900 (6-8 US cents) per kilogramme. He calculates that his costs for fertiliser, seeds, pesticides and electricity for irrigation alone were Dong 800 per kilogramme. Nonetheless, Quang admits that he is living and eating better now than before the economic reforms began in 1986.

Houses in the north are tightly clustered in villages surrounded by bamboo hedges, while dwellings in the south are scattered along the Mekong river's tributaries. That, according to Vietnam observers, has played a key role in shaping the different worldviews of peasants in the two halves of the country.

"In the north, the bamboo hedge determines the village," observers Tran Van Giau, a southern historian. "It keeps villagers in and outsiders out. If you have no fence, you have no limitations. People who produce a lot are more liberal than those who live inside a bamboo hedge."

Giau says southern peasants are more susceptible to outside influences because they do not have fences. For example, early French missionaries were more successful in finding Roman Catholic converts in the south than in the north. In the north, their first converts were traders and fishermen who lived outside traditional, fenced-in Confucian villages.

The openness of the Mekong delta also has spawned support for several indigenous religious sects that gained a foothold earlier this century. Quang follows the Hoa Hao religion, a reform Buddhist group with about two million members founded by a prophet/faith-healer earlier this century. Other southern farmers adhere to the Cao Dai religion, an eclectic movement claiming Victor Hugo, Joan of Arc, Jesus Christ and Buddha as its saints. Neither group has attracted any followers in the north.

Pimps and Panhandlers

Ho Chi Minh City looks a lot like old Saigon

HO CHI MINH CITY — The police who raided Bambi Cafe in Ho Chi Minh City in April 1992 quickly discovered that owner Nguyen Thi Tot had too zealously pursued the Communist Party's new gospel of free-market economics.

She operated the cafe as a brothel with over 100 prostitutes. Worse, Tot had even infiltrated pimps into guesthouses belonging to the Ministry of Interior, the army and the police department — the backbone of the city's security apparatus.

Finding that her best customers were businessmen and tourists from Taiwan, Hongkong and Singapore who were willing to pay US$500 or more for virgins, Tot hired cosmetic surgeons who "restored" the girls' virginity for future high-priced service. Tot also had a network of tailor shops and other businesses to camouflage her real money-spinner.

Bambi Cafe is only the latest symbol of how much the new Ho Chi Minh City is beginning to look like the old Saigon. Police told journalists reporting Tot's exploits that the city today has 50,000 prostitutes, up from 40,000 when the communists took over in 1975.

The red banners that a decade ago exhorted people to build a socialist paradise have been replaced by huge billboards advertising Sony video players, Tiger beer, Citizen watches and 555 cigarettes from the capitalist world. Hordes of child pickpockets, handicapped beggars and panhandlers selling anything from used postage stamps to pornographic playing cards overwhelm any foreign visitor brave enough to leave his hotel on foot.

Growing numbers of homeless people sleep on the streets outside restaurants and nightclubs where the city's *nouveaux riches* often drop up to US$1,000 for a single night's party. Drug addicts — thought by the police to number around 30,000 — openly shoot heroin and peddle opium in a run-down park near the city's main Ben Thanh market.

"I can't predict what Ho Chi Minh would say if he were still alive," Deputy Mayor Pham Chanh Truc says. He attributes the city's social problems to uneven economic development, unemployed migrants from the countryside and the "negative" side of the country's open-door policy.

Although few statistics are available, economists estimate the city accounted for nearly 20% of the country's exports and 27% of its imports in the first six months of 1992, even though less than 7% of Vietnam's population lives there. Its two-way trade of US$422 million was more than 10 times that of Hanoi.

Despite critical electricity shortages, Ho Chi Minh City accounts for a full third of Vietnam's industrial production and 70% of its output of consumer goods. Ho Chi Minh City in the five years prior to mid-1992 had captured 197 foreign investment licences capitalised at US$1.2 billion. This is more than 40% of the foreign capital pledged for the whole country and over half of all foreign licences issued.

Ironically, northerners have played a key role in the south's economic revival. Some of them fled the communist take-over in the north in 1954 and became a major force in the southern economy during the US war. Many of these people have resumed their business activities since the party began abandoning socialist economics in the mid-1980s.

Others are northerners who have arrived since 1975, including some who were sent to implement Hanoi's Draconian policies. One example is Le Van Kiem, who was born in Hue in the centre, but fled to the north in 1947 to join the anti-French resistance. He was sent to Ho Chi Minh City in 1975 to work as an engineer for a state transport company and liked what he found in the south.

Kiem quit his government job and invested some of the

wealth his family had acquired as former gold merchants to establish what has become the biggest and most modern private garment factory in the country. Huy Hoang Co. in 1991 exported US$10 million of jackets, mainly to Germany.

"The fixed idea that northerners don't know how to do business just isn't true," argues a journalist in Ho Chi Minh City. "They need time to learn, but after that they'll catch up."

Ho Chi Minh City's nearly 400,000 ethnic Chinese provide another economic impetus. Although many are still reluctant to invest their own capital, they are proving to be an important conduit for investment from Taiwan and Hongkong.

Despite Ho Chi Minh City's free-wheeling atmosphere, it has not proven to be a capitalist paradise. "Many foreign businessmen see Saigon as the El Dorado, and then have their fingers bitten off," observes the representative of a foreign trading company working in both parts of the country. "It's more difficult to get into the north, but it's easier to get into trouble in the south."

Ho Chi Minh City has more capitalists than communists.

Defeated by Victory

Military faces crisis in wake of budget cuts

The army may not even be able to maintain equipment.

HANOI — The abrupt loss of aid from the former Soviet Union in 1991 increased the troubles facing Vietnam's once-formidable army just when it was struggling to adjust to peace and the collapse of its longstanding communist allies. China's forward advances in the disputed South China Sea in the wake of the Soviet empire's demise exacerbated the worries facing Vietnam's generals.

Even before the Soviet Union disintegrated, Vietnam's military — which humiliated three of the world's strongest armies in the past four decades — had been weakened by the country's own economic difficulties. These problems have played havoc with the army's plans to overhaul its structure, demobilise half its troops and halt declining morale and standards among its ranks.

Moscow had underwritten most of Hanoi's military expenses for more than 30 years. Neither Hanoi nor Moscow has released figures on the value of past Soviet military aid, but Western intelligence agencies estimated that it totalled roughly US$1 billion a year at the height of Vietnam's occupation of Cambodia.

During Vietnam's war with the US, Moscow provided Hanoi with most of its arms and ammunition. After China attacked Vietnam's northern border in early 1979 in retaliation for Hanoi's invasion of Cambodia a few weeks earlier, Moscow helped expand Vietnam's air force and navy and stepped up its training of military officers.

The Vietnamese army will now be hard-pressed to service its Soviet tanks, aircraft and naval vessels, many of which are already aging and far less sophisticated than the hardware possessed by its neighbours. "In a year or two, the Vietnamese could face a serious problem in maintaining their equipment and getting spare parts," says a diplomat who monitors the Vietnamese military.

Maj.-Gen. Vu Xuan Vinh, director of the Ministry of Defence's external relations department, says the army will now be forced to expand its own poorly developed defence industry, which currently produces only rifles, machine guns, rocket launchers and ammunition.

Officer and specialist training also will become more difficult for the armed forces, which had borrowed heavily from Soviet military doctrine since the early 1970s. Moscow, which had as many as 1,000 military advisers in Vietnam in the early 1980s, withdrew its last expert in May 1992. The former Soviet Union already had stopped accepting new Vietnamese military students three years earlier.

Moscow's aid cuts, coupled with the withdrawal of Russian air and naval forces from the Vietnamese base at Cam Ranh Bay, will force Hanoi to reassess its defence strategy, which long counted on Moscow's support in the event of hostilities with China.

Neither Russian nor Vietnamese officials are willing to disclose Russia's current force levels at Cam Ranh. "The numbers keep changing," Vinh said in late 1992. "But their numbers now are only one-tenth of what they were before. Only a few planes and small ships remain. Only a few hundred people stay there, compared to tens of thousands before."

In early 1990, US officials said the Soviets had 14 Tu16 bombers, 14 MiG23 fighters, several Tu95/142 anti-submarine and reconnaissance aircraft and an average of 15-20 warships and support vessels at the base.

Although Vietnam and China normalised their relations at the end of 1991, Hanoi's generals have watched with alarm as Peking had advanced its claims in the South China Sea in the wake of Russia's withdrawal from Cam Ranh and the American pullout from its bases in the Philippines.

In early 1992, China's national assembly passed a law on territorial waters claiming all islands, including the Spratly archipelago disputed with Vietnam and four other countries, in the South China Sea. In May, Peking signed an agreement with Crestone Energy Corp. of the US to explore for oil in an area Hanoi claims is part of its southern continental shelf.

A month later, Chinese troops landed on a reef in the Spratlys claimed by Vietnam and established what Peking called a "sovereignty post." Then in September, Vietnamese officials charged that a Chinese oil-drilling rig had been positioned in the Gulf of Tonkin, only 130 kilometres off the coast of northern Vietnam.

Hanoi's military leaders say they are still trying to assess the country's geopolitical position and ascertain the army's future strategic requirements in light of Vietnam's withdrawal from Cambodia, the collapse of communism in the Soviet Union and the continuing territorial disputes with China.

A Vietnamese Communist Party Central Committee plenum, meeting in June 1992, reopened a debate on whether China remains a long-term strategic threat to Vietnam's security. But party leaders reportedly were unable to agree whether to classify China as having "expansionist" designs in the region.

Nonetheless, the central committee appears to have given in to the cash-starved army's request for at least some additional funds in response to the territorial dispute with China. Deputy Premier Phan Van Khai told the National Assembly in September 1992 that the government had faced "additional expenses in coping with new complicated developments along the border and in the [South China] Sea."

Although the Vietnamese navy has quadrupled in size since 1975, its equipment is no match for the Chinese fleet. Vietnam's navy had only seven old Soviet and American frigates, 64 patrol boats and seven amphibious craft, while China is building a blue-water navy that has 94 submarines, 19 destroyers, 37 frigates and 869 patrol and coastal combat vessels, according to the *Military Balance 1991-1992*, published by the International Institute for Strategic Studies (IISS) in London.

"We will have to upgrade our navy and air force to protect our sovereignty," Vinh says. "But we're poor, so we can't buy much modern equipment. We'll have to do it gradually."

But the general adds that Vietnam would have to rely primarily on diplomacy to counter further Chinese advances. "If China uses its modern weapons to invade the Spratlys, it will not only have to consider the reaction of Vietnam but of other countries, as well," he says, referring to several Asean countries that also claim part of the archipelago. "I'm sure the US will not let China expand so much."

The army, which often blames the collapse of communism in the Soviet Union and Eastern Europe on foreign intervention, sees the other potential threat to Vietnam as subversion from the capitalist West, particularly the US.

In a speech to an army conference in May 1992, Defence Minister Doan Khue told his audience that "imperialist forces have lent a helping hand to those reactionary Vietnamese in exile overseas so that they can establish contacts with a number of discontented, degenerate and deviant elements at home and have them circulate books and papers calling for pluralism and a multi-party system and undermining the unity and single-mindedness in the party and among the people."

Hanoi's top-ranking general warned that Vietnam's opponents "have called for the depoliticisation of the army in a bid to deprive the party of its leadership role and overthrow the people's administration."

Vinh says any internal uprising against the party is the responsibility of the Ministry of Interior's security police, and "the army would only get involved if the opposition forces have weapons." Diplomats report that several crack northern military units were sent to Ho Chi Minh City in 1990, when the party feared possible political demonstrations around the time of the 15th anniversary of the communist victory on 30 April.

Vietnam's own economic crisis had forced deep cuts in the military budget, even before the Soviet Union collapsed. In late 1989, then defence minister Le Duc Anh complained to the National Assembly that the military had received only two-thirds of the budget approved by the Communist Party's politburo. He said that more than 70% of the military budget was spent on feeding and housing soldiers, leaving less than 30% for maintaining and procuring equipment.

"Owing to the lack of funds for building storage facilities and for maintaining and repairing weapons and equipment, a lot of technical equipment of various types was left in disrepair," Anh told parliament. "Unless the equipment is promptly repaired and regularly serviced, some of it will have to be discarded. That would mean losing armaments that are worth billions and not easy to buy even if money is now available."

In recent years, Hanoi's official media have been filled with articles complaining about the shortage of food, housing, medicine and uniforms for soldiers. In early 1991, Lieut-Gen. Dam Van Nguy, military commander along the border with China and a member of the party Central Committee, told the *People's Army Saturday* magazine that "the living standard of our soldiers everywhere in Vietnam is too bad, too terrible, and has produced a negative impact on their work, study, training and combat preparedness."

Dam said his troops complained they did not have enough

Disabled veteran runs a market stall.

energy to train all morning after eating only one bowl of rice for breakfast. Because of low military pay, many of them had to depend on extra money from their families to survive.

Vietnam's official newspapers regularly report that the army's economic difficulties have caused a sharp increase in corruption and smuggling by soldiers. In late 1990, the party newspaper reported that military units at the Long Binh military depot, where US equipment captured at the end of the war in 1975 is stored, "have misappropriated national property worth tens of billions of dong over the past 10 years."

Military units along Vietnam's borders with China and Cambodia are also involved in the smuggling. "Some army units and ranking military officers involved in smuggling rings often use military vehicles to transport trafficked goods," the official *Saigon Giai Phong* daily reported in August 1992. "In some cases, armed soldiers have even escorted these vehicles and used weapons to resist any attempts by law-enforcing officials to inspect their vehicles." Other press accounts complain of officers misappropriating their troops' provisions, army units destroying forest preserves and the theft of private property by soldiers.

"Vietnam's economic problems are hitting the army and demoralising its troops," one diplomat observes. "Before they had a national cause to liberate their country. Now personal survival is at stake."

Nevertheless, he warns against under-estimating the Vietnamese army. "It's still an army to be reckoned with — it's a very war-experienced army. Motivation can quickly be brought to the country at a time of crisis," he says.

Since the 1989 withdrawal of Vietnamese soldiers from Cambodia, Hanoi has demobilised half the army and deployed many units to carry out civilian and infrastructure-related work projects. Vinh says the number of regular armed-forces personnel, including air force and navy, has been cut by 600,000 men since 1986. Their numbers in 1979 were estimated at 1.2 million.

However, demobilising more than half a million troops has proved a difficult task. Few of the retiring officers have the skills to compete in Vietnam's labour market, which is already suffering from unemployment estimated by the Asian Development Bank at around 20%. Some of the demobilised troops have been organised into economic units, while others returned to school. Some also left to work overseas before the foreign labour market in Eastern Europe and the former Soviet Union began drying up in the late 1980s.

Troop cuts have not yet reduced the military's expenses, often estimated by foreign observers at one-third to one-half of the national budget. "The transition costs a lot of money in the first few years, but we hope we can save money later when the [former] soldiers help increase production," says retired Gen. Tran Van Tra, the commander who oversaw the surrender of the former South Vietnamese government in 1975.

The army's revamped force structure will emphasise "a standing force which is numerically small but high in quality, combat-efficient and constantly modernised," Gen. Nguyen Quyet, the former director of the army's political department, told Radio Hanoi in 1989.

Officials say the standing army is backed by a massive

local militia. There is also a reserve corps, estimated at around 3.5 million by the London-based IISS.

"If there's a new war, we'll carry out people's defence," says Lieut-Gen. Hoang Phuong, director of Vietnam's Institute of Military History, referring to the strategy used so effectively against France and the US.

Vietnam's military first launched its modernisation programme — under which weapons were to be upgraded and standardised and former "political generals" were to be replaced with younger, professionally trained officers — shortly after the defeat of South Vietnam. In the early 1980s, Hanoi stepped up its efforts to train a more professional officer corps and abolished the "dual-commander system" that provided for power to be shared between officers and political commissars. The reforms meant that more autonomy was given to military commanders.

But Vietnam's economic troubles have made it harder for the armed forces to find students for its officer-training academies. In recent years, the military's elite Institute for Science and Technology near Hanoi has had difficulty finding even half of the qualified students required to fill the 100 slots in its first-year class.

Further, Radio Hanoi reported in 1990 that desertion rates among recruits were high due to "poor political knowledge" and "fear of hardships and a life of privations." Another report said 50% of those of military age in the northern city of Haiphong had failed to report for medical exams, while 20 high-ranking officials had helped their sons evade conscription.

In December 1990, the National Assembly reduced the term of military service from three years to two years — except for air force and naval personnel — in an apparent attempt to woo young men worried about spending too much time away from the civilian job market. Vinh says the shorter terms of service also will allow more young men to get military training. Analysts say the military is focusing its recruitment drive in the countryside, where people are more accustomed to harsh living conditions than in urban areas.

Soldiers of Fortune

Making money is easier than making war

HANOI — The Truong Son Corps has switched from making war to making money.

The corps is best known for its exploits in building the Ho Chi Minh trail, along which Hanoi infiltrated troops and military equipment from the north to the south during the Vietnam War. But instead of cutting roads through jungle-covered mountains and replacing bridges knocked out by US bombers, the corps is now producing tools, laying railway tracks and growing coffee — all for profit.

The Vietnamese army has been involved in such activities as building roads and opening up "new economic zones" and state farms in remote, unpopulated areas since the defeat of the Saigon government in 1975. But during Vietnam's march towards socialism in the years that followed, there was little concern about cost or efficiency.

By the mid-1980s, with the economy on the brink of bankruptcy, the Vietnamese Communist Party was forced to introduce wide-ranging market-style reforms. No longer able to afford its huge and unproductive army, Hanoi gave military units permission to set up companies and begin doing business for profit.

The Truong Son Corps, headed by Do Xuan Dien, was one of the first to accept the challenge. In April 1988 it turned itself into the Truong Son General Department of Construction. It now has 19 different enterprises involving projects such as the construction of the D'ray H'ling hydroelectric power station in the Central Highlands, extracting

Not just soldiers, but businessmen.

and exporting marble and mining coal in the northeastern province of Quang Ninh.

In 1990, Dien says the company earned a profit of more than Dong 5 billion (then worth US$600,000), a healthy sum considering its lack of business experience and the troubled state of Vietnam's economy. The Ministry of Defence took 30% and Truong Son reinvested most of the rest to upgrade its equipment.

Truong Son's 7,000 or so employees earn an average of Dong 110,000 a month, nearly twice the salary of most soldiers, though Dien insists his workers have not forgotten their roots. "We're still members of the army, so if there's a war we're ready to jump back into the battlefield," he says.

The company, which earlier built Highways 7 and 9 in Laos using aid funds from the former Soviet bloc, is looking both for work abroad and joint ventures with foreign companies inside Vietnam. One of Truong Son's enterprises recently signed an agreement with a Japanese firm to extract and export 20 million cubic metres of local sand for use in renewing Japanese beaches.

Dien says he has also signed a memorandum of understanding to build a fish market in Australia and has begun negotiating with a US firm interested in investing US$30 million to produce bananas for export. "But because of the

US trade embargo, discussions are proceeding slowly," he says.

The Vietnamese army in 1991 had 62,000 soldiers, or roughly 10% of the standing army, working full-time for about 60 companies and enterprises set up following a March 1990 Council of Ministers' decree allowing the army to go into business. Local militia units have set up another 160 enterprises, according to Lieut-Gen. Phan Thu, director-general of the Defence Ministry's General Administration of Economy and Technology, which advises units interested in beginning commercial activities.

The navy has taken up fishing, while the air force is flying foreign oil officials to offshore exploration rigs. Other military units are involved in logging, aplite and tin mining, repairing ships and growing rubber and coffee. Some factories that used to produce military equipment have switched to making consumer goods, such as electric fans and bicycle parts.

Vietnamese military officials will not disclose how much of the Defence Ministry's income is generated by these activities. But in 1985, Le Trong Tan, then a senior general, said the army raised just under 20% of its revenue from internal sources.

Soldiers in regular military units are also being encouraged to become involved in money-making ventures when not involved in training. Many units have set up livestock farms and brick kilns, while others are growing rice to supplement their Defence Ministry budgets. "They use their profits to improve their food or build new barracks," Thu says.

But not all military-cum-business units are doing so well as Truong Son. In a 1991 interview published in the *People's Army Saturday* magazine, Col. Trinh Dang Quang, general director of the 3rd Corps' Red River General Co., complained that he often missed business opportunities because he lacked decision-making power and frequently had to wait up to a year for approvals from the ministry. He also complained that the equipment his company inherited was "backward," making it difficult for his products to compete on the market.

Confined to Barracks

Army's political influence is slowly eroding

HANOI — In late 1990, hundreds of letters began arriving at the Vietnamese Communist Party headquarters in Hanoi calling for the re-election of Nguyen Van Linh and Do Muoi, then respectively party chief and premier, at the seventh party congress in June 1991.

Although top party leaders undoubtedly appreciated the letters' message, they ordered a halt to the campaign after they discovered it had been orchestrated by a group of army veterans.

Party officials apparently feared that some of the country's 4 million veterans — and perhaps some serving soldiers

New marching orders: stay out of politics.

— were trying to exert political influence as a military bloc. Although the army is one of three key Vietnamese political institutions, its direct influence ranks far behind that of the party and the government apparatus.

Despite this, the armed forces remain the most popular institution in Vietnam, particularly in the countryside. Many appreciate the sacrifice of the army during the country's recent wars, and believe the military has managed to maintain closer relations with the population than the party or government since the return of peace.

The Vietnamese army has been under strong party control ever since Vo Nguyen Giap and 33 revolutionaries equipped with 31 rifles and two revolvers united to form an armed propaganda team in December 1944. The military has remained subordinate to the party ever since.

Although some differences emerged between the party and the army on such questions as the speed of the Vietnamese troop withdrawal from Cambodia in the late 1980s, major conflicts have never erupted publicly. Carlyle Thayer, a Vietnam specialist teaching at the Australian National University, attributes this to the fact that many officers are party members who have been indoctrinated to accept that the party has veto power over the military command. In a 1986 study, Thayer estimated 90% of the officer corps and more than one-third of the army's rank-and-file were party members.

Party chief Linh reminded the military of its role as a servant and protector of the party at an army conference in Ho Chi Minh City in December 1990. "We have concentrated on building the army politically, trying to ensure its political steadfastness in the face of the complicated situation at home and abroad," he said, alluding to Vietnam's economic crisis and the collapse of communism in Eastern Europe. "This is to enable it to perform satisfactorily its duty of protecting the party, the socialist state and national independence."

Most of the political influence exerted by Vietnam's officer corps comes through their overlapping party and government jobs. Two members of the current 13-man ruling Politburo are serving generals.

The army also has "bloc membership" on the party's central committee, though its size generally has been falling in recent years. The current central committee, elected in 1991, has 14 active army officers, or 10% of the total. Thayer notes that the military held 8% of the seats in the 1986 central committee, compared with 13% in 1982 and 16% in 1976.

The army also has long served as a recruitment base for the party. Although recent figures are not available, US Vietnam expert Douglas Pike estimates that six of 10 new party members recruited in 1975-82 were from the armed forces. Thayer estimates that by 1986 the army accounted for 14% of the party's membership, which then totalled 1.8 million members.

"It's easier for people who serve in the army to join the party," says Maj.-Gen. Vu Xuan Vinh, who heads the Defence Ministry's external relations department. "The army is a big school for training party members."

But because Vietnamese commanders have no local power base, unlike their Chinese counterparts, it has been possible for the party to dismiss some of the army's most prominent war leaders. Giap, architect of the defeat of the French at Dien Bien Phu in 1954, was ousted from the politburo in 1982 — apparently for criticising Vietnam's invasion of Cambodia and Hanoi's tilt towards Moscow during the Sino-Soviet split. Gen. Van Tien Dung, who masterminded the offensive that defeated the Saigon regime, lost his politburo post in 1986, allegedly for corruption.

Most Vietnamese and diplomatic observers view the army, or at least its senior officers, as a conservative force in the country's politics. While a large number of younger officers are said to be strong supporters of the party's economic and political reforms, many high-ranking military officials are worried such moves could lead to social chaos. Shortly after the party began the reforms in 1986, then military chief of staff Lieut-Gen. Doan Khue, who has been promoted to minister of defence, warned that too much attention to economic development could "hurt the thinking and feeling of those who have taken up weapons."

The Persian Gulf War in 1991 prompted a new round of anxiety among many senior officers. "We should not lay emphasis on national construction alone [because] building the country must be accompanied by defending the country," Lieut-Gen. Doan Chuong told Radio Hanoi a few weeks after the fighting stopped. "Now there is an external manoeuvre to eradicate socialism in the region. And it is certain that this manoeuvre will be accelerated more vigorously."

Despite these warnings, many Vietnamese believe the influence of the army in politics has declined gradually in recent years. "Two things have reduced the role of the army — the Cambodia withdrawal [in 1989], including the decision to demobilise a large number of soldiers, and the lessening of tension along the Chinese border," one civilian official observes.

The army's fear that the party is reducing its emphasis on national security has prompted at least some protests from the armed forces. In January 1991, Radio Hanoi reported that some local military congresses, meeting in preparation for the national party congress, complained that the party's new draft platform said little about building the army, "thus leaving everyone with the impression that the armed forces have been downgraded and national defence has been deprived of its significance."

But even if the role of the army is downgraded, its 4 million veterans will continue to be a powerful force in Vietnamese society. Since 1975, tens of thousands of veterans have been given leadership positions in many party and government organisations and state enterprises as rewards for faithful service. But civilians often complain that the promotion of veterans, most of whom lack the managerial skills needed in the civilian market, is an important cause of the current inefficiencies in Vietnam's economy.

Uncle of the Nation

Was Ho Chi Minh a nationalist or communist?

He probably wouldn't recognise today's Vietnam.

LANG SEN, Nghe An — They placed burning joss sticks in the traditional ancestor altar urn and knelt silently before a bronze bust of a wispy-bearded old man. These dozens of young people had been hand-picked to come to this child-hood home of Ho Chi Minh, the founding father of indepen-dent, communist Vietnam. With bowed heads, they listened as their achievements and failures were recited for Ho's departed spirit.

Nineteen-ninety was the year of remembering and honouring Ho Chi Minh, and the ceremony in the village of Lang Sen in Nghe An province was just one of many events marking the nationwide celebration of the 100th anniversary of Ho's birth, which was commemorated on 19 May.

In Ho Chi Minh City, formerly Saigon, Diep Minh Chau, one of Vietnam's best-known sculptors, carved an 8-metre, 200-tonne white marble bust of the venerated revolutionary. Chau, a 74-year-old southerner who lived with Ho for six months in the mountains of north Vietnam in the early 1950s, says the task was more difficult than he had thought. "It's hard to depict Ho," he says. "He was so full of determination, yet he was a very simple person."

In Hanoi, the Russians, who then were still Vietnam's most important patron, built a massive Soviet-style museum to exhibit Ho's personal belongings, including his frayed Chinese-style jacket and famous sandals cut from a rubber tire.

"Uncle Ho wouldn't have wanted all this fuss on his birthday," says Nguyen Sinh Que, one of a handful of Ho's surviving relatives in Lang Sen Village. In 1959, when the army bought materials to build a museum in his childhood village, Ho ordered the supplies to be used for building a school instead, Que says.

More than two decades after his death, Ho's image as the venerated uncle of all Vietnamese who rallied his country to oust the French and the Americans remains largely intact, despite the cynical view that many Vietnamese have adopted towards Ho's disciples since the end of the war in 1975.

Homage to Uncle Ho is a common feature of daily life, particularly in the north. Hundreds of people line up outside the Soviet-built mausoleum in Hanoi each day, waiting for a brief glance of his embalmed body. Pictures of the slightly smiling former president hang in all government buildings and in most shops and homes, while schoolchildren grow up on stories about his exploits in the struggle for independence.

Vietnamese, however, differ in their assessment of why Ho is so revered. Tran Van Giau, a French-educated historian who was ousted by Ho as leader of the southern communist movement in 1945, says the former president is most remembered for his humanism. "Ho took people as the centre of his activities," says Giau. "He's like a person who founded a new religion."

Nguyen Huy Thiep, one of the most controversial and widely read writers in Vietnam today, insists Ho is popular for the economic improvements he brought to people's lives. "Before this, people suffered constant hunger," he says, referring to Ho's programme to distribute land to landless peasants in the 1950s. Now, says Thiep, "many leaders pay too much attention to Ho as a spiritual leader, but the people don't understand much about independence."

But for younger people, who are more interested in improving their living standards than they are in politics, Ho has become a distant historical figure, Thiep says. "For the generation after me, his image has faded. They only know Ho as the president of the republic," he says.

Vietnamese party officials, clinging to one-party rule while their former Soviet and East European allies have abandoned communism, are using his popularity to mobilise public support at a time when public cynicism against the party is increasing.

Party leaders lace their speeches with references to Ho as the founder of the party, quoting Ho to rail against corruption, abuse and incompetence among party members, and often conclude by declaring that "the great president Ho Chi Minh will live forever in our cause."

But Ho's legacy is also used by critics of the country's current leaders. "After the death of Ho Chi Minh, my people and I are afraid the leadership took the wrong way," says archaeologist-historian Tran Quoc Vuong. "In 1945, Ho sent a letter to local provincial committees saying that if the nation got independence but the people were not happy, then independence meant nothing," Vuong says.

Others criticise the party for abandoning Ho's delicate

39

foreign policy balancing act. Tran Bach Dang, the Communist Party boss of Saigon during the war against the US and a frequent critic of Hanoi's post-war policies, believes China went to war with Ho's disciples in the late 1970s because they had abandoned Ho's policy of trying to balance relations between the communist giants at the time, China and the former Soviet Union.

Several years ago, some newspaper articles charged that Ho's successors had doctored his last will and testament after the president died. To end the speculation, the party Politburo published his last statement and admitted that Ho's wish to be cremated and his request for a one-year moratorium on farm taxes had been ignored.

Although the party and Ho's disciples are often criticised, no doubts have been raised about Ho, at least in public. He has escaped the harsh scrutiny and disillusionment that has befallen other revolutionaries like Stalin and Lenin in the former Soviet Union and, to some extent, Mao in China.

The scores of Vietnamese scholars researching his life follow the party's lead in depicting Ho as a near-mythical figure. Some scholars reportedly have begun using modern research techniques such as analysing Ho's handwriting, but their findings have not been made public.

Despite the official adulation for Ho, his closest colleagues readily admit that he made mistakes in leading the revolution. "If we say Ho made no mistakes, this is only in our imagination," says Vu Ky, a long-time personal secretary of the former president.

Ho's most frequently mentioned "mistake" is the radical land-reform programme carried out in the mid-1950s, and in whose name thousands of landlords and rich peasants were killed. Ho publicly apologised for the excesses and fired his party chief, Truong Chinh.

"It's not correct to say the land reform was a mistake — it speeded up the war against France," Ky says, referring to the fact that the programme prompted thousands of poor peasant children to join Ho's army. "But in the course of its implementation, some wrong methods were used."

Many details of Ho's life, particularly during his first 50 years, remain sketchy, although the recent opening of the Comintern archives in Moscow to foreign researchers and journalists should provide additional details. American writer Sophie Quinn-Judge found records in these files showing that Ho was not quite as ascetic as he is often depicted by Hanoi's propagandists.

Quinn-Judge found records indicating that Ho, at least for a time in the 1930s, was married to Nguyen Thi Minh Khai, a Vietnamese revolutionary who was killed by the French in 1941. But, according to the party's official history, Khai was married to another revolutionary, Le Hong Phong.

People who worked most closely with Ho say he rarely talked about his past, and unlike Lenin or Mao, he wrote down few of his ideas. "You should understand Ho through his actions," says Giau, who characterised Ho as a pragmatist.

Ho grew up in Nghe An province, which had a long tradition of opposition to Chinese domination and French colonial rule, but the date of his birth is uncertain. The date officially has been set as 19 May 1890, though one French secret-police report said it was 24 January 1892 and his first visa request to visit the former Soviet Union listed it as 15 January 1895.

Ho's father was a Confucian scholar who was removed from his position in the royal court for his anti-colonial leanings. Ho's mother died when he was 10, and his older brother and sister were imprisoned for their activities opposing French rule.

Ho was named Nguyen Sinh Cung at birth, and at 11, he was renamed Nguyen Tat Thanh. As a young man, Ho changed his name to Nguyen Ai Quoc, or Nguyen the Patriot. Historians in Hanoi claim Ho used 76 different pseudonyms during his lifetime. Ho Chi Minh, the last name he adopted, means "he who enlightens."

In 1911, Ho left Saigon aboard a French ship, which had hired him to work in the kitchen. Hanoi's official history has it that Ho travelled to the West to find ideas to use to oust the

French. "Once I have seen how they do it, I will come back to help our compatriots," Ho was supposed to have told a friend before he left.

Ho spent the next 30 years abroad, much of it in the former Soviet Union and China. He also took odd jobs in New York and London, before moving to Paris, where he painted fake Chinese ceramics and retouched photographs for a living. His failure to get a hearing at the 1919 Versailles conference, at the end of World War I, convinced Ho that independence could only be won through violence.

Ho joined the French Socialist Party and began reading Lenin's writings, which he later claimed provided the key to Vietnam's independence. "Though sitting alone in my room, I shouted aloud as if addressing large crowds: 'Dear martyrs, compatriots, this is what we need, this is the path to our liberation'."

In 1924, Ho went to Moscow, where he joined the Communist International, the Soviet organisation promoting worldwide communist revolution. The Comintern sent Ho to southern China, where he set up a Youth League and taught Marxism-Leninism to young Vietnamese who had fled to China to escape the French police.

Under instructions from the Comintern, Ho united three rival communist groups into the Indochinese Communist Party during a meeting at a soccer field in Hongkong on 3 February 1930. But soon a split developed in the party between intellectuals like Ho, who gave priority to the struggle for national liberation, and those who supported the Comintern's line calling for a socialist revolution first.

Ho lost his position in the party, which openly criticised his emphasis on national independence as a "*petit-bourgeois* hangover." In 1931, Ho was arrested in Hongkong, and after his mysterious escape from a prison hospital some 18 months later, he reappeared in Moscow.

Little is known about Ho's time in the former Soviet Union, but scholars now believe that he was ordered to remain in Moscow as punishment for his "mistakes," and that he may have even been put on trial by the Comintern.

In 1938, after Stalin agreed to allow colonised countries to struggle for national independence, Ho was sent back to southern China to work with Vietnamese communists. Three years later, during the Japanese occupation, Ho returned to Vietnam for the first time in three decades and founded the Viet Minh, a patriotic front to fight for independence.

Ho quickly captured the hearts of many Vietnamese with his simple lifestyle and direct speech, his attention to social grievances, and his ability to explain his revolutionary aspirations using traditional Confucian symbols, says historian David Marr in his book,*Vietnamese Tradition on Trial, 1920-1945*.

Ho also quickly demonstrated his ability as a "master of clandestine operations, a skilled analyst of international affairs, a shrewd judge of lieutenants, a patient designer of political consensus," Marr writes.

After Japan's surrender in August 1945, Ho declared independence and founded the Democratic Republic of Vietnam, with himself as president. But French troops — backed by the US — soon returned, prompting Ho to launch a guerilla war, which finally led to the defeat of the French at Dien Bien Phu in 1954.

But at a peace conference in Geneva, the world's major powers divided Vietnam, giving Ho control only of the northern provinces. Vietnam was soon back at war, with the communist north, supplied by the former Soviet Union and China, fighting the US-backed south. Ho died on 2 September 1969, nearly six years before his successors defeated the south and reunited Vietnam.

The 30-year US effort to block a victory by Ho's northern army over the south begs one of the most puzzling questions of his life: was Ho a patriot first who used communism as a vehicle to struggle for independence, or was he an international communist disguised as a patriot?

Ho's colleagues insist he was both. "Ho came to communism starting from patriotism," says Nguyen So, the director of Ho's museum in the city named after him. "Then Ho realised the liberation of one country can't be separated from

43

the liberation of other countries, so he became a cadre of the Comintern."

Despite his years of work with the Russians, Ho turned to the US rather than to the former Soviet Union, for support for his independence struggle after he returned to Vietnam in the early 1940s. He cooperated with US intelligence officers operating in northern Vietnam during World War II, and his declaration of independence on 2 September 1945 began with a quote from Thomas Jefferson's declaration of independence for the 13 American colonies.

Over the next 18 months, Ho sent 11 telegrams and letters to Washington appealing for US support, but none of his messages were acknowledged. In late 1945, Ho officially "dissolved" his Communist Party, leaving only "study groups," hoping to attract sympathy from the West.

Ho's appeal for support from Moscow, which had shunted him aside in the 1930s for being more a patriot than an internationalist, also went unanswered. "I place more reliance on the US to support Vietnam's independence, before I could expect help from the USSR," Ho told Archimedes Patti, an American intelligence officer who had frequent contacts with Ho in 1945. Moscow did not recognise Ho's resistance government until 1951.

But it is impossible to say what kind of political system Ho would have established in a reunified Vietnam. His successors are foundering these days as they debate how to respond to the dismantling of the communist parties in the former Soviet Union and Eastern Europe. This confusion makes it difficult to assess Ho's impact.

"Ho's legacy can be used in different ways," says an American Vietnam specialist. Thus, reformers use Ho to promote liberalisation, while conservatives cling to his role as founder of the party as a way of promoting communist orthodoxy.

The scholar speculates that Ho's legacy will be the emergence of a Vietnamese "socialism with a human face," that will be pragmatic and open. "That is the only way the party will maintain the respect of the people."

Reaching Out

Vietnam seeks to end its isolation

HANOI — The landing of the Boeing 747 carrying French President Francois Mitterrand at dilapidated Noi Bai airport on 9 February 1993 marked a major step away from Vietnam's international isolation.

The first Western head of state to visit Hanoi since Vietnam gained independence from the French in 1954 cheered his hosts by promising to increase aid and publicly urging the US to lift its trade embargo.

But Mitterrand also irritated the country's fiercely independent leaders by warning them that they need to take further steps toward democracy and expand civil liberties if they hope to see their economic reforms succeed. "There cannot be economic opening without political opening, and it's an illusion to think other-

President Le Duc Anh.

wise," the French leader declared during a speech at a dinner hosted by Vietnamese president Le Duc Anh.

Despite his criticisms, Mitterrand also had some strong words for the US. "Just one piece of advice: get rid of the embargo," he told journalists. Since Vietnam withdrew its troops from neighbouring Cambodia in 1989, Paris has campaigned to restore Hanoi's eligibility for loans from the International Monetary Fund, suspended in 1985 under pressure from the US. On 2 July 1993, the US announced it would no longer oppose the loans.

"The Vietnamese must be very pleased with the first visit by a Western head of state," one diplomat observes. "Until now, everything has been bubbling in a regional sense, but Mitterrand's visit is Vietnam's most important coming-out toward the West."

Vietnam launched its campaign to end more than a decade of international isolation when it signed the Cambodian peace agreement in Paris in October 1991. Within a few weeks, Hanoi had taken major strides towards repairing its strained relations with most of the world, particularly China and the Association of Southeast Asian Nations (Asean), which had led a campaign to isolate Vietnam after its 1978 invasion of Cambodia.

The Communist Party's seventh congress in June 1991 had abandoned ideological considerations as the dominant driving force in Hanoi's foreign-policy deliberations. Facing growing chaos in the Soviet Union, which had long bankrolled Vietnam's backward economy, the party began stressing that Hanoi wanted to be "a friend of all countries in the world community."

Without Soviet backing, Hanoi was forced to drop its long-standing objections to a UN-sponsored peace agreement in Cambodia. The signing of the Cambodian peace accord, which ended 13 years of Vietnamese hegemony in Cambodia, prepared the way for the rapid improvement of Hanoi's links with the outside world.

Some Vietnamese analysts believe the Cambodian agreement marked a dramatic shift in Hanoi's strategic thinking. "In the past, Vietnam never used diplomacy as a weapon against China, France and America," a former diplomat explains. "It became impossible to use diplomacy because we had the habit of thinking that only armed force solves problems."

With the collapse of the former Soviet Union, the Communist Party realised its survival depended on the success of its economic reforms. "The seventh congress stressed that the top priority of our nation was to develop our economy," Deputy Foreign Minister Le Mai says. "To achieve a favourable environment, we need to carry out a policy of diversifying our international relations."

Hanoi also for the first time began stressing relations with its Asian neighbours, although debates continued within the leadership on whether to focus on China or on Vietnam's non-communist neighbours in Southeast Asia. "People with some attachment to China emphasise that China and Vietnam are socialist countries facing ideological subversion from the West," a Vietnamese foreign-policy analyst observes. "Pragmatists say countries which were enemies of Vietnam — Asian, America and Japan — can become our friends."

Despite Hanoi's campaign to find new friends, party leaders continued to warn against allowing expanded foreign ties to disrupt the party's monopoly hold on political power. "While opening wide our door to attract and welcome investment, technology and management experiences from foreign countries and to expand the world market for our products, we must strive to maintain political stability and national security," party chief Do Muoi warned a party Central Committee plenum in June 1992.

Perhaps the biggest boost to Vietnam's economy came from Japan's announcement in November 1992 that Tokyo would resume low-interest credits to Vietnam. Japan, the last industrialised nation to honour the US embargo, had suspended its aid programme 14 years earlier following Hanoi's drive into Cambodia.

Tokyo's first commodity loan totalled ¥45.5 billion (US$370 million). Japanese officials expect this to be followed in 1993 by the resumption of project credits to develop the country's dilapidated infrastructure, particularly its roads, seaports, telecommunications network and airports. Hanoi hopes the Japanese credits will help revive an economy still struggling to recover from the loss of assistance from the former Soviet Union and from years of stagnation caused by mismanagement and a US-led aid embargo.

The resumption of Japanese aid is expected to prompt a sharp increase in investment by Japanese companies, which are attracted by Vietnam's substantial natural resources and potential to become a low-wage production base. Even though Japan had emerged as Vietnam's second-largest trading partner after Singapore, Japanese companies had remained reluctant to invest because of fear about angering the US.

Prior to Tokyo's loan announcement, Vietnam had expected bilateral aid of less than US$200 million in 1992. Much of this was provided by other US allies, including France, Italy, Britain and Australia, which had resumed modest aid programmes to Vietnam after Hanoi withdrew its troops from Cambodia.

In late 1992, Washington took further steps to ease its trade embargo against Vietnam in response to its stepped-up efforts to account for some 1,700 American servicemen still listed as missing in action (MIA) since the end of the Vietnam War in 1975.

During an October 1992 visit to Hanoi by special US presidential envoy Gen. John Vessey, the Vietnamese government announced that it had begun a nationwide search of its archives for documents and photographs related to the missing servicemen and would turn over its findings to Washington. President George Bush called Hanoi's pledge a "real breakthrough" in the search for the MIAs and declared that "finally, I am convinced that we can begin writing the last chapter of the Vietnam War."

Two months later, Bush announced that US companies would be allowed to open offices, hire staff, conduct feasibility studies and negotiate contracts pending the full lifting of the embargo. Earlier in the year, Washington modified its trade embargo to allow the resumption of direct telecommunications links between Vietnam and the US.

In regional affairs, a summit between Chinese and Vietnamese party and state leaders in Peking in November 1991 officially ended more than a decade of cold war between the world's two most populous communist countries. Vietnam had long sought rapprochement with China, but Peking held

Communist Party chief Do Muoi.

Hanoi at arms length until its alliance with the Soviet Union had collapsed and the Vietnamese had signed the Cambodian peace accord.

Since the summit, a flurry of Chinese and Vietnamese officials have exchanged visits, the two countries have restored air links and Chinese companies have begun exploring trade and investment opportunities in Vietnam. But the restoration of relations has fallen far short of the high-minded

49

goal of some Vietnamese officials who had hoped for fraternal ideological support following the disintegration of Soviet communism.

Normalisation was troubled by decades-old bilateral differences, particularly over competing claims in the South China Sea and a poorly defined land border. In February 1992, China's National Assembly passed a law on territorial waters claiming all islands, including the Spratly archipelago disputed with Vietnam and four other countries in the South China Sea.

In May, Peking signed an agreement with Crestone Energy Corp. of the US to explore for oil in an area Hanoi claims is part of its southern continental shelf. A month later, Chinese troops landed on a reef in the Spratlys claimed by Vietnam and established what Peking called a "sovereignty post." In September, Hanoi charged that China had begun illegal oil exploration in an area of the northern Gulf of Tonkin claimed by Vietnam.

Vietnamese officials said they feared that China was taking advantage of the departure of American and Russian naval forces from Southeast Asia to step up pressure on its southern neighbour and fill the vacuum left in the region. Following cutbacks forced by the loss of Soviet aid, Vietnam's military lacked the capability to respond to advances from China, which was in the process of beefing up its air force and navy.

Alarmed by China's moves, Vietnam's Central Committee — meeting in a plenum in June 1992 — reopened a debate on whether China remained a long-term threat to the country's security. But Vietnamese officials say the party was divided over whether to classify China as having "expansionist" designs in the region.

Chinese Premier Li Peng's December 1992 visit to Vietnam, the first by a Chinese leader in 21 years, failed to resolve the territorial disputes. Li declared that the "common points between Vietnam and China outweigh and outnumber their disputes," but Vietnamese officials insisted that many problems remained unresolved.

The Chinese premier used his presence in Hanoi to try to calm fears in Southeast Asia that China was attempting to fill a power vacuum in Asia left by the collapse of the Soviet Union and the withdrawal of US forces. He told his Vietnamese hosts that "China will never seek hegemony nor practice expansionism."

But Hanoi candidly voiced its continuing reservations about Peking's intentions. "We took note of the statements," Foreign Minister Nguyen Manh Cam told journalists. "It is our hope that they will be translated into reality."

The Cambodian peace accord also led to dramatic improvements in Hanoi's relations with its non-communist neighbours. Premier Vo Van Kiet mounted a major fence-mending trip to Indonesia, Thailand and Singapore in October 1991 after the peace agreement was signed. Kiet's trip ended four days before he accompanied party chief Muoi to the summit in Peking, suggesting that some Vietnamese officials were looking to Asean to help counterbalance Chinese influence in Southeast Asia.

Early in 1992, Kiet, who was the first Vietnamese premier to tour Asean since 1978, visited Malaysia, Brunei and the Philippines. In July, Vietnam signed the Treaty on Amity and Cooperation, often called the Bali treaty, which granted Hanoi observer status in Asean and marked Vietnam's first step towards becoming a full member of the group.

"Relations between Vietnam and Asean have great potential," says Deputy Foreign Minister Le Mai. "Our economies are complementary, we are near to each other and the standards of commodities are similar."

The most important leg of Kiet's late-1991 Asean tour was the premier's visit to Singapore, which ended more than a decade of suspicion and animosity. In the months that followed, Singapore, which emerged as Vietnam's largest trading partner following the disintegration of the Soviet Union, dropped its restrictions on investment in Vietnam by Singapore companies and opened an embassy in Hanoi.

The two former adversaries signed a host of agreements on shipping, aviation, trade and investment protection, and

Singapore became increasingly active in helping Vietnam develop plans to upgrade its infrastructure and protect its environment. In April 1992, Singapore's senior minister and former prime minister, Lee Kuan Yew, who long campaigned to isolate Hanoi, visited Vietnam to advise government leaders on their path from central planning to market economics.

Kiet's visit to Thailand, followed by then Thai premier Anand Panyarachun's trip to Hanoi in early 1992, marked another important step in Vietnam's efforts to improve its links with its Southeast Asian neighbours. Hanoi's relations with Bangkok over the past four decades had been more tense than with the other Asean countries because of Thailand's active support for the US war in Indochina and for the guerillas fighting Vietnam's occupying army in Cambodia.

During Anand's visit, he offered Vietnam long-term credits worth Baht 150 million (US$5.8 million) to purchase Thai goods and services, and the two sides signed a protocol updating their 1978 agreement on trade, economic and technical cooperation. Hanoi also agreed that Thailand could set up a consulate in Ho Chi Minh City.

The highlight of the visit was to have been the signing of a joint fishing-cooperation agreement, but Vietnam withdrew the draft accord two days before Anand arrived. "Vietnam has many fishermen using only poor technology, so the government must look after the conditions of these people to make a living," Deputy Minister Mai said, explaining why Vietnam had pulled out of the agreement. "Nobody rejects some kind of cooperation, but the question is how do you have cooperation which is beneficial to both sides."

Malaysia also actively courted Vietnam. Malaysian Prime Minister Datuk Seri Mahathir Mohamad, accompanied by more than 100 businessmen, visited Hanoi in April 1992 to promote increased investment and trade between the two countries. Mahathir's delegation signed several economic agreements in Hanoi, including a memorandum of understanding on Malaysian assistance to Vietnam's rubber industry.

Dynamics of Despair

Minorities struggle to escape poverty

SAPA — Hanoi's free-market reform programme has brought few benefits to Tan Sanmay, a Dao minority woman who farms on the steep mountain slopes of Lao Cai province near Vietnam's border with China.

The 53-year-old grandmother says the biggest change brought by the reforms is that the village cooperative has been abandoned.

What little cultivatable land there is in Ta Phi village has been divided among individual families. But with the demise of the cooperative, farmers no longer have access to government-subsidised fertiliser to boost their output. Sanmay, who is illiterate, is not sure how much land her family farms, but she estimates her plot produced enough rice last year to feed her family of nine for eight or nine months.

Sanmay, who like most minority women works 14 to 15 hours a day in the fields and cares for her family, moved to Ta Phi when she got married at 15. "After that I gave birth to a child every year, or at least two in every three years," she says. Sanmay had a total of 12 children, five of whom died of various illnesses when they were young.

The village administrative office has a small clinic but no medicines. The nearest hospital offering treatment for malaria and the severe stomach disorders that afflict the people of Ta Phi is 12 kilometres away on foot in the district town of Sapa.

Sanmay tries to send her two youngest children to school for a few hours early in the morning before they have to help in the fields, but the village has had trouble keeping its teachers. "They come for one or two months and then they leave," she says. "Often we have no teacher for several months."

Life in Sanmay's village, as in other minority communities in the northern mountains and central highlands, is harsh. A government economist estimates that the living standard of minority villages in Vietnam is only one-fortieth of the level in Hanoi.

Vietnam's 53 ethnic minority groups total roughly 8 million people, or about 11% of the country's 71 million population. The 10 largest groups — the Tay, Thai, Hoa (or ethnic Chinese), Khmer, Muong, Nung, Hmong, Dao, Jarai and Ede — each number from 100,000 to 1 million people. The six smallest groups have less than 1,000 people each.

Apart from the Hoa — who mainly live in Ho Chi Minh City and lowland towns — and the Khmer — who live in the southern Mekong River delta — most of the other minorities dwell in the northern mountain and central highland regions that comprise about 75% of Vietnam's land area. These regions are of key strategic importance for Hanoi as they contain most of the country's forest and mineral resources.

The minorities' centuries of relative isolation ended abruptly in the 1940s, when the Vietnamese communists launched their war of independence against the French colonialists. Vietnamese revolutionaries established their resistance bases in highland areas, where they recruited minority soldiers, while the French co-opted some groups to fight for the colonial army by promising them autonomous zones.

During Vietnam's war with the US, the highland areas were heavily bombed and sprayed with chemical defoliants — particularly on the central plateau — further disrupting the lives of the minorities living there. More trouble came in 1979, when China launched its invasion of northern Vietnam in areas inhabited mostly by minorities.

After the communist victory in 1975, they ploughed most of their meagre resources and limited foreign aid into developing industry in the cities and agriculture in the fertile Red and Mekong River deltas.

The minorities, many of whom practise shifting cultivation in or at the edge of the country's forests, were encouraged to resettle in fixed communities and become self-sufficient in food production, a goal that proved unattainable. Most villages continue to face rice shortages for three to nine months each year.

Rapid natural population growth among minorities, coupled with the migration of several million ethnic Vietnamese from the overcrowded deltas to the highlands in the late 1970s and early 1980s, resulted in a severe land shortage in the region. The unrelenting search for food has led to the rapid destruction of the country's forests and a sharp loss in soil fertility, further reducing the ability of minority farmers to eke out a living.

As the Communist Party began its drive to establish a free-market economy in the mid-1980s, however, it abandoned its emphasis on local food self-sufficiency. "We now realise that if you plant industrial or cash crops, they can be exchanged for food," says Hoang Duc Nghi, the minister in charge of mountainous areas and minority affairs. "But first you need to solve the transportation problem. How do you shift to a market economy without roads?"

Hmong farmers in Bac Ha district near the Chinese border have begun planting plums, apricots and other fruit on their terraced hillside fields, but because of the lack of roads they get poor prices for their produce in the Red River delta.

The highlands also face other infrastructure problems. Because most highland provinces have no electricity, annual per-capita consumption totals only 18 kilowatt hours. For example, Pleiku, one of the biggest cities in the central highlands, has no telephone links with the outside world.

Despite the poverty of the highlands, they have many of the country's most promising natural resources. Most of Vietnam's rapidly dwindling forest reserves are located in the central plateau, while the northern highlands have vast untapped mineral resources, including coal, iron ore, phosphate, bauxite, tin, gold, silver and precious stones.

The former Soviet Union recognised the central plateau has ideal soil conditions for raising rubber, coffee, tea and other cash crops, but political and economic chaos forced the Soviets to abandon their projects in the late 1980s. The best sites for building hydroelectric dams to alleviate the growing energy shortages in the southern provinces are also located in the central highlands.

A Politburo resolution in 1989 put new emphasis on developing the country's minority regions and integrating them into the national economy. The government has organised a series of conferences around the country to discuss strategies to develop the country's highland areas, but Hanoi is desperately short of funds.

Gia Lai province in the central highlands expected to receive only Dong 15-16 billion (US$1.4-1.5 million) from the central government in 1992, most of which was earmarked for education and health, according to deputy provincial governor Hoang Le. Hanoi in 1991 invested only about Dong 100 billion in the highlands, roughly 15% of its capital investment budget, says Tran Tho Nghi, deputy director of the State Planning Commission's Department for Localities.

The lack of government help for highland areas has created some resentment. "We only received a certificate saying that we had made a great contribution," complains the party chief of a minority village west of Danang, which had supported the communists during the war with the US. "We haven't received any aid from the government since 1975."

One of the biggest changes under communist rule has been an attempt to legislate racial equality and elevate more minorities to government and party posts. In 1991, Nong Duc Manh, a member of the Tay tribal group and the head of the Central Committee's ethnic minorities commission, became the Politburo's first minority member.

The party's 146-member Central Committee includes 13 minorities, while 163,000 party members, 7.5% of the total, come from minority groups. The National Assembly has 66 minorities among its 395 representatives, but most civil servants in highland areas are still ethnic Vietnamese because the pool of literate minorities is so small.

Some minorities feel that their equality exists mainly on paper and that many local officials and ethnic Vietnamese continue to look down on them. "The state's policy against discrimination is correct, but people who carry out the policies in the provinces, districts and villages don't follow this policy," complains a minority village party chief. "They say we lack education, live in caves and eat salt. I think discrimination has increased since 1975."

Some minorities are also worried about the government's post-1975 policy to encourage lowland farmers to set up new economic zones in the highlands in an attempt to reduce population pressures in the deltas. Out of Gia Lai province's current population of 720,000 people, for example, roughly 200,000 are lowland Vietnamese who have arrived since the end of the war.

Land disputes have erupted periodically between the minorities and the newcomers, and these tensions appear to have increased since the party abandoned farm cooperatives in the late 1980s and began moves to divide land among individual families.

Dai Doan Ket magazine reported in 1992 that many minorities in Lai Chau province in the northwest were demanding the return of their former ancestral lands. In an effort to resolve the disputes, the article said that several thousand ethnic Vietnamese had been forced to leave the province and return to their former homes in the Red River delta.

The shortage of arable land in the northern mountains also has prompted some minorities to migrate south. Since the late 1980s, tens of thousands of Hmong and Dao farmers have moved from areas bordering China to provinces south of Hanoi and to the central highlands, where they have often become embroiled in land disputes with the local population. *Nhan Dan,* the partly daily, reported that in 1990 and the first half of 1991, some 85,000 minority people had moved from the far north to Song Be province, northwest of Ho Chi Minh City, where they were accused of destroying 5,000 hectares of forest.

The party's recent moves towards a free-market economy also appear to have spawned an increase in opium production, particularly in the northern mountain regions. Recent visitors to Son La province on the Laotian border report seeing opium growing openly along the main roads.

"In the past, people only grew opium for family use, but now they can sell it on the market so they produce more," says Hoang Ngoc Lam, the Hmong police chief in Lao Cai province's Sapa district.

Nghi believes that Vietnam's northern provinces produced roughly 15 tonnes of opium in 1991. Lam says apart from some opium used for local consumption, much of the crop is smuggled out through China and the Vietnamese port city of Haiphong. Foreign narcotics experts say some is also moved through the international airports of Hanoi and Ho Chi Minh City. Nghi says the government is interested in foreign aid to introduce alternative crops, but he believes it will be difficult to stamp out opium cultivation unless roads are built to move bulkier produce to market.

Government and party officials admit they can do little to improve life in the highlands and capitalise on the area's vast economic potential without outside help. "We recognise that we have to lean on the mountain areas, which have forests and a potential for industrial crops and mining, to develop our economy," a government economist says. "But our biggest problem is the lack of capital."

The mountain areas have so far attracted little foreign investment and aid, though a few firms from South Korea, Singapore and Japan have begun investing in wood processing and silk production in the central highlands. One reason for limited investment is clearly the region's poor infrastructure. But another key obstacle has been the government's refusal to allow all but a handful of foreign businessmen and aid workers to visit the central plateau due to fears of possible unrest caused by minority insurgents.

Vietnam has so far largely escaped the separatist unrest among its minorities that continues to plague the former Soviet Union and even China, though an insurgent group known as the United Front for the Struggle of Oppressed Races (Fulro) mounted occasional attacks in the central highlands after 1975. The group, which had earlier received funding from France and the US to fight the communists, said its goal was to establish an independent nation for minorities.

Officials in Gia Lai say most of Fulro's members had surrendered or fled the country by 1985, but a 1991 article in the army newspaper *Quan Doi Nhan Dan* suggested that at least some rebels continued to operate for much longer.

Victims of Neglect

Minorities are plagued by lack of education

Hmong children at school in Trung Chai.

PLEIKU — Only two of the 96 Bana ethnic minority families in A Luk village near Pleiku in the central highlands send their children to the neighbourhood school 2 kilometres away. Villagers say they need their older children to help in the fields, and keep the younger ones home because they fear they could get hurt by logging trucks as they walk to school.

Vietnam has made impressive gains in educating its lowland population in recent decades, but its minorities still lag far behind. According to 1989 census figures, illiteracy among the Bana stands at 80%, far higher than the national average of only 12%. But for the Hmong of the northern highlands, the figures are even more dismal. Only 10% of the group's members — and 3% of its women — can read and write.

Only about 12,000 of 400,000 school-age Hmong children currently attend school, says Deputy Minister of Education Tran Xuan Nhi. In the central highlands the figures are somewhat better, with 5,200 out of 57,000 school-age Jarai children attending school.

Of the minority children who do go to school, only a tiny proportion are girls. "We have the traditional idea that a boy belongs to us and a daughter to someone else," says Giang Seo My, a Hmong and head of the Women's Association in Lao Cai province. "When she grows up she will get married and join another family. Until then, we keep our daughters at home to help with housework."

Nhi says the shortage of teachers poses another problem. He estimates that only 20% of the teachers in the highland areas are minorities themselves or ethnic Vietnamese who come from highland areas. "Even if we offer teachers salaries of five to seven times higher than that offered to teachers in the lowlands, they don't want to go to the highlands because the living standards are so low and it's so easy to get sick," he says.

To tackle this problem, the Education Ministry has begun setting up boarding schools in highland areas. Nhi says four such schools have been set up at the national level, 31 at the district level and 100 in larger villages. The advantage of boarding schools is that they can serve a scattered population with limited staff, but the disadvantage is that the cash-short government cannot afford to run them.

Officials readily admit that the government's curriculum, developed for ethnic Vietnamese, is often irrelevant to the lives of minority children. These children are particularly disadvantaged because Vietnamese, a language unknown to all but a handful of them, is the medium of education. Nhi says his ministry is trying to introduce teaching in minority languages in the fourth grade, but acknowledges this is difficult because only 12 of the 54 languages in the country have a written form.

The highlands also pose unique health problems. The incidence of malaria, which had been reduced sharply in the 1960s and 1970s, has been rising since the mid-1980s in the central highlands and areas bordering Laos and Cambodia, says Health Ministry official Dr Le Duc Chinh.

One reason is that malaria in these areas has become resistant to known drugs, Chinh says. Another is that Vietnam has lost its supplies of cheap pesticides from the former Soviet Union. The Health Ministry in 1990 recorded nearly 140,000 known cases of malaria, which resulted in 3,340 deaths.

Goitre, caused by iodine shortages and believed to reduce its victims' intellectual capacity, also plagues minority areas. Dr Trinh Tuyet Nhung, who heads Lao Cai province's health department, says 41-43% of the province's population suffer from goitre, compared with only 3-4% of people living in the Red River delta.

Although the Vietnamese Government claimed by the late 1980s to have increased nationwide immunisation coverage for children under one year to over 70%, children in the highlands still lag far behind. In Gia Lai, 54% of the children under five have received some vaccinations, while in Lao Cai the figure is only 52%, according to local health officials.

Despite growing land pressures in the highlands, the government's family-planning efforts in the region so far have met with almost no success. The army newspaper *Quan Doi Nhan Dan* reported in early 1992 that the birth rate in Lao Cai province's Bac Ha district, a predominantly Hmong area, stood at 5%. That compares with the nationwide average of 3.2% and the urban rate of 2.3%. The paper attributed the high rate in part to the fact that 30% of the district's girls were married by the time they were 14 years old.

Cultivating Trouble

Slash-and-burn farming is alive and well

LAO CAI — Resettling migratory slash-and-burn farmers has been the cornerstone of Hanoi's policy towards its minorities as it seeks to save what is left of Vietnam's rapidly dwindling forests. Since 1968, 1.9 million of the country's 2.8 million shifting cultivators have been resettled.

But the programme has had only limited success in stabilising the lives of those resettled, says Ma Chuong Tho, deputy director of the Forestry Ministry's Fixed Cultivation and Sedentarisation Committee. Of those resettled in fixed villages, some 70% continue to practise slash-and-burn farming.

"The government lacks capital to build public projects like irrigation networks, roads and schools, so people keep moving," Tho says. "The population in the highlands is increasing so rapidly that we don't have enough land in the lowlands for them."

A forestry report prepared by the United Nations Food and Agricultural Organisation argues that pressure on land in the highlands is so intense that slash-and-burn farming is no longer a sustainable form of cultivation. The report says that land shortages are causing shorter fallow cycles.

Land scarcity also threatens what remains of the country's forest cover. Forests covered 44% of Vietnam in 1944, but this figure had fallen to about 24% by the early 1980s, according to Forestry Ministry officials. In Lao Cai province alone, forest cover has fallen from 240,000 hectares 15 years ago to 123,000 hectares at present, says Dang Quoc Long, head of the province's Forestry Department. Of this lost cover, 80-90,000 hectares of forest were felled by shifting cultivators.

Deforestation has created 9.7 million hectares of barren hills in northern Vietnam, posing serious environmental hazards. For example, officials blame two devastating flash floods in Son La and Lai Chau provinces in 1991 on the destruction

Farming, yes. Deforestation, no.

of mountain forests. In addition, soil erosion and silting threaten many agricultural irrigation systems.

In an attempt to limit the destruction of the country's remaining forests, Hanoi introduced a ban in January 1992 on the export of raw logs — extended in March to include rough sawn timber. It is not immediately clear, however, what impact the ban will have on the country's forests. A journalist who visited Gia Lai in the central highlands three months later counted 63 trucks loaded with raw logs travelling from Pleiku to the port city of Quinhon during a two-hour period.

Local officials insisted the trucks were carrying logs cut prior to the ban or imported from neighbouring Cambodia or Laos. But many officials in Hanoi are worried that local officials and logging company executives, who have long profited from timber exports, will find ways to circumvent the ban.

Logging company officials in Gia Lai and Lao Cai say the recent bans would force them out of business because they lacked capital to invest in equipment to process wood or produce furniture. Highland officials are also concerned that the new regulations will wipe out their most important source of foreign exchange. Gia Lai's exports in 1991 totalled only US$8 million, most of which was earned from the sale of 20,000 cubic metres of raw logs.

The government's reforestation efforts have so far proven only partially successful. During the past decade Lao Cai has replanted 20,000 hectares of trees, of which only 6,000 hectares have survived.

To give farmers greater incentives to care for newly planted trees and protect the remaining forests, Hanoi launched a scheme in 1988 based on distributing one-third of the country's 19 million hectares of forest land to individual families in 35-50 hectare lots. But Long thinks the new policy will have only a limited impact on mountain areas. "We don't have enough land for agriculture," he says. "We first need to help people be self-sufficient in food. Only then can we protect our forests."

The Drop-Out Factor

Education crisis follows economic reforms

HO CHI MINH CITY — Vietnam's communist authorities, who shut down private social-welfare programmes in the southern provinces after seizing power in 1975, are once again turning to the private sector to rescue the country from a deteriorating education system that is suffering from a growing number of dropouts and falling morale.

At the Vinh Son Roman Catholic Church in Ho Chi Minh City, the Daughters of Charity of St Vincent de Paul have opened three classes for 77 street children ranging from six to 15 years old. "We want to give them an education and prevent them from becoming beggars or thieves," says Sister Beatrice My, who administers the group's small education programme.

The Daughters of Charity, who run five private schools for 358 homeless children around the city, provide each child with lunch and two changes of clothes using funds raised from local supporters and from their headquarters in Paris. "If I don't give them food their parents won't let them go to school," My says. They need the children to earn money for their food.

My readily admits that her programme helps only a tiny fraction of the city's school dropouts but the Catholic sister says she lacks funds to expand her classes. Cao Minh Thi, director of Ho Chi Minh City's department of education and training, estimates that at least 60,000 of the city's children aged between six and 11 are not attending school.

Saigon Giai Phong, Ho Chi Minh City's official daily

Catholic school helps to rescue education system.

newspaper, in 1991 reported that some 2.2 million Vietnamese could not read or write. It also reported that 1.2 million children nationwide from six to 10 years of age had dropped out of school, along with another one million between the ages of 11 and 14.

Education Minister Tran Hong Quan says that the country's economic difficulties, coupled with the government reforms giving people greater freedom to make money, had increased the school drop-out rate in this Confucian society, which has long prized education.

"We're entering a market economy . . . so many families want their children to work at an early age," Quan says. "Our education does not provide work skills, so when students reach secondary and high school, people don't see the benefit of studying."

Despite these problems, most educators laud the government for its efforts to expand the country's education system since the defeat of French colonial rule in 1954. Quan says Vietnam's current education crisis has to be compared to the situation in 1945, when the country had only 16 lower secondary schools, three high schools and three university classes.

Now the country has 15,000 primary and lower secondary schools, 1,080 high schools and 102 colleges. In 1945, he said, 90% of the population was illiterate, while today nine-tenths of the people can read and write.

"This mass education system exceeds the ability and strength of our economy," Quan says. "This has affected the quality of our education." The minister says the government had increased spending on education from 6.7% of its budget in 1986 to 12% in 1991, but he acknowledges that actual spending per student had decreased because of the country's rapidly growing population.

Cao Minh Thi, Ho Chi Minh City's education director, says his department receives only Dong 50,000 (US$4.50) per student each year. The city spends three-quarters of its education budget on teachers' salaries, leaving little money for new equipment and supplies.

The average teacher earns only about Dong 60,000 a month, compared with salaries of well over Dong 100,000 in the private sector. Thi says that several thousand teachers resigned in recent years because they could no longer make ends meet, while those remaining were forced to look for second jobs. Many parents complain that most teachers no longer teach basic lessons during regular school hours, but insist that students come back for special after-hours tutoring sessions for which they are charged extra fees.

"We need to ring an alarm about the poor funding for education, or we risk having a lost generation," says Thi.

In some provinces, Quan says, teachers are leaving their jobs more quickly than new ones can be trained. "Because of the lack of teachers we have to use school graduates with only a few months' training," he says.

Teacher training institutes are also finding that the country's talented young people are no longer interested in entering the teaching profession, which once enjoyed high prestige. "Our college doesn't attract the best students because they find the living standard of teachers too low," says Do Quang Ninh, deputy director of Ho Chi Minh City's Secondary School Teachers' Training College.

Most Vietnamese educators and parents say the quality of education has declined sharply in the past decade. Vietnam began upgrading its curriculum in 1981 to put greater emphasis on vocational training and technical and scientific skills, but Ninh says the economic difficulties of teachers have prevented most of them from mastering the new material.

Teachers say many students are also suffering from a crisis of motivation. Because of the country's low salaries and high unemployment rate, graduates often have to spend several years looking for jobs after they finish school. "The quality of students arriving from secondary school is very poor," says Dao Cong Tien, the rector of Ho Chi Minh City's Economics University. "They don't have enough background to enter university."

Vietnam's poverty also affects graduate students granted scholarships to study abroad. *Nhan Dan*, the party's daily newspaper, reported in 1991 that many students going overseas spend most of their time trying to make money rather than studying. In 1990, 80% of Vietnamese students abroad asked for extensions to complete their studies.

To pull the country's educational system out of its nosedive, the government several years ago began charging school fees and allowing private schools to open. These reforms would have been considered heretical when the communists came to power and declared free, state-funded education for all as a key tenet of their domestic policy.

Students in cities are expected to pay fees ranging from Dong 8-15,000 per month, at least on paper. But parents complain that wide-scale abuse of the fees has emerged in many schools. The official news agency's *Vietnam Weekly* reported that some schools in Hanoi charge students 17 or 18 different fees.

Alarmed by the deteriorating quality of public-sector schooling in the whole country, a group of teachers and scientists recently established the first private school in Ho Chi Minh City to train the city's most talented children.

Other teachers have organised a semi-private secondary school and a private university to teach students who have failed to qualify for state-funded institutions.

The Tri Duc private secondary school opened in June 1991 with two senior primary grade classes — for children of about 12 years old — and 20 part-time teachers. From 200 applicants, the school chose the 80 children who scored highest in a rigorous entrance examination. Over the next few years, the school plans to expand the number of classes through to pre-university levels.

"Our goal is to train experts in science, technology, industry, economics and health," says Tran Van Hao, principal of the new school and one of its founders.

Although the school follows the general curriculum developed by the Ministry of Education, it has been adapted to stress technical skills, particularly in mathematics, computer science and foreign language training, especially English. The teachers have rewritten the turgid state-supplied lesson texts — which in most schools are simply memorised — to try to stimulate student creativity through activities such as mathematics games.

All of the teachers have full-time jobs in other schools or scientific institutes around the city. Hao, for example, teaches mathematics at the Teachers' Training College and heads its computer centre. To give teachers time to prepare their lessons, they are paid Dong 100,000 a month — roughly the salary of a full-time professor at a state college — for eight hours of teaching.

The school is financed by student fees of Dong 80,000 a month, more than five times that of state schools. Even so, the fees do not cover the school's operating expenses. The school cannot afford its own building or equipment, so it rents several rooms from a public school and computer equipment from the Teachers' Training College's computer centre.

In the state sector many colleges and universities supplement their income by setting up small businesses. Ho Chi Minh City's Economics University, which receives state scholarships for only 260 of its 12,000 students, raises half of its budget by providing consultancy services for local businesses and organising visits for foreign tourists and academics to Vietnam.

Dao Cong Tien, the university's rector, says the country's education crisis will be reversed only when the cash-strapped government stops trying to subsidise education for all children. "We should mobilise people who can afford to pay for education," he argues, pointing out that the private sector has profited much more than the state budget from the Communist Party's economic reforms. "The state should continue subsidising only the poorest students," Tien maintains.

No Jobs for The Boys

Many youths face long-term unemployment

HO CHI MINH CITY — Every Sunday night hundreds of youths on motorcycles descend on the centre of town for a little *chay long rong* — cruising down Dong Khoi Street.

Once known as Tu Do Street, American soldiers used to come here to drink and pick up girls during the Vietnam War. The "bikies" swing right at the Saigon River and come back around the block in a ritual that can go on for hours.

The main purpose appears to be to show off their Honda Dream motorbikes, Vietnam's current status symbol, flirt and pick out dates for the next weekend. Those taking part, however, are very much a minority of young Vietnamese — the children of the politically powerful or those whose families have made money since the communist government modified its doctrinaire socialism.

For the majority of young Vietnamese people, finding a job, rather than showing off a motorbike, is their biggest consideration. The government abandoned its utopian pledge of providing jobs for everyone in the early 1980s, when mismanagement and an international aid embargo following Hanoi's invasion of Cambodia nearly bankrupted the country.

Although the Communist Party has given more freedom to the private sector, it is still too small to absorb the 1.2 million young people who enter the job market each year. Most of them say they have to look for at least three to five years for their first job, and some say they have been looking for more than a decade without success.

Computer training might help them get jobs.

Ho Chi Minh City has no exact statistics on unemployment, but a Vietnam News Agency report in 1991 said it totalled 230,000, of whom 80-90% were young people. The number of under-employed — those with only part-time jobs — is several times higher.

Vietnam's economic reform has brought an explosion of imported consumer goods, which has fuelled a sharp increase in consumerism among young people. Parents are worried that this is leading to a breakdown of traditional values. "The market economy has provided more rice and many new houses, but it has brought too much competition into society," says a father raising three children in Hanoi. "Sometimes I'm nostalgic about the old days when we were poor but human relations were good."

The growing expectation of youth for more consumer goods leads to frequent family tensions at a time when Vietnam remains one of the world's poorest countries. "Children want more beautiful clothes, cosmetics and shoes than their fathers or mothers wear," says Nguyen Khac Vien, a French-trained paediatrician who runs a small private centre for child psychology in Hanoi. "This creates conflicts in the family

73

because parents don't have enough money."

Vien says family poverty — coupled with boredom resulting from Vietnam's lack of recreational facilities — is also driving more young people to engage in crime to get money to buy what they want.

Vietnam's official media frequently warn about relaxed sexual attitudes and increasing alcohol and drug abuse among the nation's youth. The army newspaper in 1991 said a study by the Institute of Hygiene and Medical Services found that 24% of the women who gave birth in Ho Chi Minh City were unmarried and most of these were under 20.

Compared to students in China, South Korea or Burma, Vietnamese young people seem to pay surprisingly little attention to politics. Students in several colleges in Ho Chi Minh City and Hanoi have organised some small protests in recent years. But they were not demanding more democracy but better living conditions and a rewriting of old Marxist textbooks that no longer fit Vietnam after it introduced market reforms in 1986.

Most young people seem more concerned about finding jobs than following contemporary political developments. Many youths interviewed in 1991 had no idea who had been elected Vietnam's new prime minister earlier in the year, though most had heard that Do Muoi had been chosen party leader in June.

Others are afraid to express their opinions. "There has been a lot of renovation in Vietnam, but if we declare a certain view and tomorrow the policy changes, we'll get into trouble," an unemployed young actor says. "It's easier to avoid politics."

The general apathy about politics is reflected in sharply declining membership of the Ho Chi Minh Communist Youth Union, once an important training ground for new Communist Party members. The union's membership had fallen from 4.2 million in 1987 to 3 million four years later.

Few youths seem interested in joining the Communist Party. Those who do often cite selfish motives rather than the idealism and willingness to make sacrifices of the previous generation.

Although most young people say they are grateful for the previous generation's dedication to the struggle to oust the French and the Americans, few, particularly in urban areas, seem interested in joining the once-admired army. Vietnam has witnessed no agitation against conscription but many young men admit they are looking for ways to avoid military service.

No Longer Paper Tigers

Press takes bolder stand on corruption

HANOI — The labour-union weekly, *Lao Dong,* published a devastating account of the alleged misdeeds of a former deputy forestry minister, including the charge that he had issued 120 fake permits for the illegal export of timber products.

The content of the article was not new; many of the details had been reported earlier and had prompted the Council of Ministers to fire deputy minister Than Trung Hieu. Readers instead were surprised by the timing of the story. It appeared a month after the Supreme People's Organ of Control and Investigation, either with the agreement of or under pressure from the Communist Party, had dropped the investigation of criminal charges against Hieu.

Lao Dong advertised its 28 November 1991 report as the first of a five-part series, but the second article never appeared. Editor Tong Van Cong says he dropped the series at the request of the court's investigating body, which asked him to turn over the newspaper's evidence after it faced increasing calls from the National Assembly and the press to reopen the Hieu investigation.

Lao Dong's decision to begin the series after the court had dropped the charges demonstrates increased courage by Vietnam's press. It also highlights attempts to improve the media's credibility since the Communist Party launched economic and political reforms in late 1986. But the newspaper's willingness to abandon the series indicates how much the press still remains a tool of the party.

Until the late 1980s, Vietnamese newspapers were generally dull and numbed their readers with endless accounts of heroic workers churning out ever greater volumes of rice or bicycles in Vietnam's march to a brighter future. One of the most striking differences today is the increasing role newspapers play in reporting mismanagement, corruption and abuse among party and state bureaucrats.

Some of these articles have landed reporters in trouble. Many, particularly in outlying provinces, have been fired and some have been arrested for reporting corruption by local officials. Reporters who in 1990 broke the story about the pending collapse of the Thanh Huong Perfume Co., which was running an illegal pyramid scheme for depositors in Ho Chi Minh City, were warned by the scheme's operator to keep quiet or face "terrible consequences."

"Before 1987, we only reported the orders of the Communist Party," says Duong Ky Anh, editor of *Tien Phong,* a Hanoi youth weekly. "Now we dare to report controversial stories about Central Committee members and provincial party leaders." Newspapers in Ho Chi Minh City reported a scandal involving the city's housing department, which in 1991 sold hundreds of government-owned villas to local officials at a fraction of the market price. Many of them made fortunes by reselling the houses.

Some newspapers have used their increased freedom to champion greater social equality. Several years ago, *Tuoi Tre,* a Ho Chi Minh City youth magazine, complained that in the selection of students for state-run colleges, priority was given to children of revolutionary families rather than to the most talented students. Eventually, the government agreed, at least in theory, to base college entrance on merit and to stop discriminating against Catholics and children from families that had supported the US-backed regime in former South Vietnam.

But some Vietnamese view the changes as largely cosmetic. "The press is a little freer to talk about corruption," says the former editor of one of the best newspapers in South Vietnam during the war. "But the newspapers just criticise small things. They never criticise government policy or high-ranking officials."

Although the press champions the party's moves towards a free-market economy, news-reporting on political or diplomatic developments has not changed much since pre-reform days. While ordinary Vietnam-ese have surprisingly ac-curate information about the workings of the party and government, this news rarely gets timely coverage in the media.

Read all about it.

Political coverage continues to follow the secretive, ortho-dox style common to Communist parties. When foreign dig-nitaries visit Hanoi, for example, the media report a long list of leaders who received the visitors but give almost no de-tails of their discussions. The leadership itself does not rely on the official media for breaking news. The Vietnam News Agency publishes two daily internal bulletins that reprint foreign press dispatches about international events and de-velopments in Vietnam. One of these is available only to the top few hundred officials in Hanoi.

Editors attribute much of the secrecy in the media to the Communist Party's 30 years of war against France and the US. "Because of the long war everything in Vietnam is con-sidered a national secret," Cong says. "After renovation, we still have not clearly defined what constitutes a national se-cret."

As communism began unravelling in Eastern Europe in late 1989, Vietnam's National Assembly passed a new press law outlawing private publications and giving the govern-ment authority to vet new newspapers and to appoint or dismiss editors. The law prohibited the press from "inciting the people to oppose the state" and from "disclosing state, military, security, economic and diplomatic secrets."

Directly or indirectly, all Vietnamese newspapers belong to the state and most, if not all, editors are trusted party members. During a media conference in Hanoi in early 1992, party chief Do Muoi reminded editors that "information must be guided" and that the press is a "shock force on the ideological and cultural front."

Muoi said that not all of the country's media have been performing their responsibilities. "There have appeared not a few press articles and books which negated the past, distorted realities and history, sowed the seeds of pessimism and advertised a pragmatic way of living, and have had negative effects on society," he said.

Prior to the reforms, editors had to clear their reports with the Central Committee's Culture and Ideology Department. But in recent years, editors say they have been allowed to decide on their own what to publish under only vague party guidelines. "We're banned from carrying articles opposing socialism or peace," says Cong, "but we're not clear what information encourages war or constitutes a struggle against socialism."

Once a week, editors meet party and government officials who brief them on how to interpret recent developments and coming events. And once a month Ideology Department officials meet editors to discuss their performance. "They directly criticise us," says Le Van Nuoi, editor of *Tuoi Tre,* one of the hardest-hitting magazines in the country. "We not only listen to their assessment, but also respond to their criticisms."

Sometimes the party does more than criticise. In June 1991, it orchestrated the removal of Nuoi's predecessor after she published an article suggesting that former president Ho Chi Minh had a wife, a view contrary to the party line.

Until a few years ago, Vietnam's press often provided valuable insights into the country's politics as reformers and conservatives aired their political differences in the newspapers. In 1990, Politburo member Tran Xuan Bach used *Tien Phong* magazine to call on the party to allow greater political pluralism, but he was soon ousted from the party's ruling body. However, with an increasing number of publications offering a greater diversity of views, the press appears in recent years to have had a less decisive role in domestic political wrangling.

Since newspapers and magazines have lost their state subsidies under the reforms, they have also been forced to turn out better quality and more attractive products. Consequently, the circulation of many publications has increased dramatically. For example, *Tuoi Tre's* circulation has jumped to 100,000 four times a week from just 30,000. Although publications have begun selling advertisements for the first time, most of their income still comes from circulation.

Press liberalisation also has led to the birth of dozens of new magazines as ministries and state institutions turn to publishing as a means to make money. Hanoi and Ho Chi Minh City each have three dailies and more than 60 weekly and monthly magazines. Most provinces also have smaller publications of their own.

In response to the competition, many publications have turned to covering sex and crime, subjects that were off-limits in this prudish communist society until a few years ago. Fearing that the number of "specialty magazines" featuring pornography, crime and astrology had gotten out of hand, the Ministry of Culture in late 1991 shut down dozens of the more sensational publications. But today even many serious publications feature scantily clad bathing beauties and report sensational murders or sex stories to attract buyers.

Answered Prayers

Religion benefits from new policy of tolerance

HANOI — The Nissan Bluebird that pulled up at Hanoi's 1,300-year-old Tran Quoc Pagoda the day before the lunar New Year carried an unlikely guest. Clad in a black Mao jacket to fight off January's chill and bearing gifts of fruit, cookies and ginseng, the secretary-general of Vietnam's Communist Party, Do Muoi, stepped out of the car and entered the temple.

Muoi chatted with the Buddhist monks for an hour, planted a tree and even allowed cameras to capture him burning incense and praying to a statue of Buddha. Two weeks later he visited the Phat Diem Cathedral, established by missionaries some 300 years ago south of Hanoi, and the country's first Roman Catholic church.

Muoi's 1993 visits to the pagoda and cathedral were the first by a senior leader of the avowedly atheist ruling party since its founder, Ho Chi Minh, contacted representatives of Vietnam's major religions in the 1940s in an attempt to build a united front to fight the then French colonial power.

Some Vietnamese view Muoi's visits as another cynical attempt by the communists to co-opt and manipulate the country's religious communities. Others, however, believe Muoi's gesture represented a peace offering to Vietnam's religious believers, with whom the party has frequently clashed since seizing power over the whole country 18 years ago.

"The visit shows Vietnam is changing," observes Thich Thanh Nha, a senior monk at the Tran Quoc Pagoda. "It demonstrates the country now has real renovation and people are free to follow religion." Muoi has "made religious believers more relaxed," adds Phan Khac Tu, a Catholic priest in Ho Chi Minh City and member of the National Assembly.

After the communists overthrew the US-backed Saigon regime in 1975, the victors moved quickly to weaken the country's religious communities as rival political forces in Vietnamese society. The new rulers knew only too well that Buddhist dissidents had played a key role in toppling the

Cao Dai priests still can't open a theological school.

southern government of Ngo Dinh Diem in 1963, while most Catholics and believers of the indigenous Cao Dai and Hoa Hao religions had actively supported Hanoi's enemies.

To prevent any new challenge to its leadership, the party took over the vast network of social institutions — schools, hospitals and orphanages — run by religious groups. Theological training schools were closed and scores of clergy were sent to re-education camps or jailed.

The party began controlling the ordination, selection and transfer of religious leaders in an apparent attempt to promote those whom it could manipulate. At the same time, the Buddhist, Christian and Cao Dai hierarchies put forward seemingly "pliable" leaders who they hoped could appease the party and limit its interference in their affairs.

But church-state tensions have eased considerably since near-economic collapse and years of international isolation forced Vietnam's communists in 1986 to adopt free-market economics and abandon old-time Marxist-Leninist orthodoxy.

By the late 1980s, most imprisoned clergy had been released and the major religions had been allowed to open small seminaries, though students are still screened by Hanoi's security apparatus.

Religious groups can once again import Bibles and publish religious books and magazines. "We still need to ask for permission to publish," Tu says, "but before if we asked for permission, we didn't get it." Religious leaders say it is now somewhat easier to transfer their clergy, build new pagodas and churches or refurbish old ones damaged by years of war and neglect. Catholic bishops can again travel to Rome and Buddhist mendicant monks have resumed "begging" for food on the streets of Ho Chi Minh City.

Lacking the funds to halt the decline in education and health services, Hanoi has also allowed religious groups to resume their social work activities. Thich Tu Giang, superior monk at the Linh Quang Tinh Xa pagoda in Ho Chi Minh City, has opened a school for 80 handicapped children in a former state-run kindergarten. Catholic nuns in the city run free schools for poor street children.

Most of the country's pagodas, temples and churches are again crowded, prompting some observers to suggest that many Vietnamese are looking for a new meaning in life following the collapse of international communism. Officials, however, reject that conclusion.

"It's not right to say people are turning to religion because they're disillusioned with communism," says Vu Quang, who heads Hanoi's Religious Affairs Committee. "Ordinary workers don't even understand what communism is."

Religious leaders differ on what they see as the impact of the party's reforms on the faith of their believers. "Formerly we had a kind of suppression of religious activities, so people were afraid to come to pagodas," says Thich Minh Chau, head of the Buddhist Research Institute in Ho Chi Minh City and a member of the National Assembly. "As the religious policy of the government has slowly opened up, people are no longer afraid to go to pagodas."

Chau believes the moral decline that has followed the party's loosening of social controls prompts others to return to their religious roots. "People are very aware that Buddhist ethics can play a role in raising moral standards, so they come back to the pagoda," he says.

But Tu believes fewer people attend church services since the reforms were launched. "Now it's very easy to go to church, but smaller numbers come," he says. "Many parents no longer let their children come to catechism because they want them to work to earn their living."

Despite improved relations between Hanoi and the country's religious groups, tensions remain. One of the main problems centres around the party's strict controls over the training and ordination of new clergy, needed to replace those who have died or fled the country as refugees over the past two decades.

The number of monks serving the country's nominal Buddhist believers — who represent an estimated two-thirds of the country's 71 million people — has fallen from about 30,000 in 1975 to roughly 20,000 today. Protestants in southern Vietnam say they have only 200 pastors, down from 500 in 1975, even though their membership has doubled to 400,000 during this time.

Unlike the Buddhists and Christians, the Cao Dai — a southern-based movement of some 2.5 million believers whose saints include Buddha, Jesus Christ, Victor Hugo and Joan of Arc — has not yet been allowed to reopen a theological school.

Many Catholic priests, particularly in the north, are forced to serve five or more scattered parishes. In addition, government officials allowed only 20 of the 43 students who completed their studies at the Ho Chi Minh City seminary in June 1992 to be ordained — even though all of the novices had been approved by the government before they began classes six years earlier.

To tackle the shortage of priests serving the country's 6 million Catholics, the Episcopal Conference sent a letter to Premier Vo Van Kiet in October 1992 asking for greater freedom to transfer priests to other areas of the country and to open new classes in the church's five seminaries.

Religious leaders also complain about harassment of their followers, particularly in remote areas. "In some regions, believers suffer from discrimination, undoubtedly because of subjective interpretation and opportunistic application of directives related to religious activities," Catholic bishops said in October 1992 in their first pastoral letter since 1980.

In February 1993, a delegation of Christians belonging to the Hmong ethnic minority in northwestern Vietnam came to Hanoi to complain that they were being harassed, beaten and fined by local officials for converting to Christianity. Minority Protestants in Gia Lai province in the central highlands say their children are not allowed to attend secondary school because of their religious beliefs.

Officials admit that such problems exist. "In the past, our enemies tried to use religion to fight the revolution, so believers and we had bad opinions of each other," says Pham Dong Giang, head of Ho Chi Minh City's Religious Affairs Committee. "Now we try to help cadres understand that the situation has changed, so our treatment of religious groups should be different."

Although large numbers of clergy have been released from prison, some are still being held. Two Buddhist scholars, Thich Tue Sy and Thich Tri Sieu, were sentenced to death in 1988 for alleged subversive activities. However, their sentences were commuted to 20 years in prison following appeals from Western governments.

Catholic priest Chan Tin and a lay colleague, Nguyen Ngoc Lan, were placed under house arrest in Ho Chi Minh City in 1990 after the priest preached three sermons calling on the government to "repent" like its former patron in the Soviet Union. Protestant sources say 16 of their leaders remain in prison in the central highlands for their alleged ties to the insurgent group known as the United Front for the Struggle of Oppressed Races.

Hanoi's most dramatic confrontation in the past year has been with Buddhist dissidents opposed to the party's formation of the Vietnam Buddhist Church. The new group was meant to replace the Unified Buddhist Church, which had been active in the south during the war in calling for peace and respect for human rights. In an attempt to silence opposition from the ousted group's leaders, Hanoi exiled its general secretary Thich Quang Do to Thai Binh in the north, and its executive director Thich Huyen Quang to Quang Ngai in central Vietnam.

But Quang, 76, launched a new round of protests against Hanoi in May 1992 during the funeral of Buddhist leader and sharp critic of the party Thich Don Hau in the central city of Hue. Quang, who remains under "pagoda arrest," staged a hunger strike to force officials to allow him to attend the funeral.

The monk spoke at the memorial service, even though he had been banned from doing so, and used the occasion to call on the regime to allow the former Unified Buddhist Church to resume its activities. The police cut off the microphone when Quang told the large crowd that the new Buddhist church had been "set up by the authorities," and had "not been elected by monks and nuns of the Buddhist clergy."

Since the funeral, the dissident monk has sent repeated letters to the government calling for the re-establishment of the earlier Buddhist church, the release of detained Buddhist clergy and the return of confiscated church buildings. In a 25 June 1992 letter, he charged that "the state-sponsored church is a political and temporary tool of the current regime which has lost its links to Vietnamese Buddhism."

Quang said the party's reforms were only "half-way measures" and declared it was impossible for Buddhists to cooperate with Hanoi, "which is inimical to religion and therefore seeks to control and intervene all the time in the internal affairs of religion." Although Quang has not been imprisoned for his scathing attacks, he has not been allowed to leave his pagoda for the past year.

Unlike China, Vietnam has never cut ties between its Catholics and the Vatican. Indeed, Hanoi's relations with the Holy See have improved in recent years. In February 1993, the Vatican's deputy foreign minister, Bishop Claudio Celli, visited Hanoi to discuss a number of disagreements.

One issue centred on finding leaders to replace two archbishops who had died and to fill two vacant bishoprics. Hanoi, which insists on approving the Vatican's appointments, rejected the Holy See's request to allow Nguyen Van Thuan, a staunch anti-communist and nephew of former South Vietnamese president Diem, to return from Rome to take up a senior post in the Vietnamese church.

The two sides also differ on whether Vietnamese priests should be allowed to participate in political organisations. Quang of Hanoi's Religious Affairs Committee says "the government cannot accept the Vatican's prohibition" against priests serving as members of the National Assembly and in organisations such as the Committee for the Solidarity of Catholics. But the Vatican, and at least some Vietnamese bishops, see the committee — which belongs to the party-sponsored Vietnam Fatherland Front — as a potential tool to control and divide the church.

"Celli's visit brought an improvement in atmosphere, but few practical results," says a diplomat.

Folk Revival

Traditional festivals make a comeback

DA TRACH VILLAGE, Hai Hung province — Vietnam's communist leaders may be proud that their six-year economic reform campaign has once again turned the country into one of the world's major rice exporters after an absence of four decades. But the peasants who grow the rice are as delighted by the relaxation of the party's earlier Draconian social controls as they are to be producing and earning more.

In early March 1993, thousands of villagers descended on Da Trach village in Hai Hung province east of Hanoi for an elaborate ceremony commemorating Chu Dong Tu, a poor 16th-century fisherman who became one of four "immortals" worshipped by Vietnamese peasants.

A long procession, including hundreds of ornately clad men and women, brought gifts of water for purification, incense, candles, flowers and food to the village temple honouring Tu. This was followed by a religious ceremony in which the villagers asked the "immortal" to bring them happiness, prosperity, longevity as well as fertility for their families and their fields.

According to a popular legend, Chu Dong Tu fell in love with the beautiful daughter of one of the Hung kings who founded Vietnam, became rich through trading with foreign countries and founded a city. The princess' father, jealous that Tu and his daughter had built a city more marvellous than his own, sent an army to destroy it, prompting the fisherman to soar to heaven and become an "immortal."

The Chu Dong Tu festival is like most of the more than

200 centuries-old folk festivals celebrated by farmers in northern Vietnam. It is a simplified version of a traditional Confucian ceremony borrowed by Vietnamese emperors from neighbouring China hundreds of years ago. All these festivals were stopped in the 1940s during the war against the country's former French colonial rulers.

Some folk festivals resumed briefly after the communist victory in 1954, but were halted again when the country's new leaders launched their brutal land-reform programme two years later. Even after Hanoi defeated the US-backed regime in the south in 1975, the party would not allow the festivals to resume, as it considered them "reactionary" and a waste of money.

Finally in 1988, two years after the party mounted its drive from a command economy toward free-market principles, Da Trach organised the first new festival honouring Chu Dong Tu. Most of the initial work was done by women, villagers say, because "they are less afraid to challenge the government."

Government officials hope their decision to allow the festivals to resume will slow the breakdown of traditional moral values. Corruption, smuggling, prostitution and drug addiction have soared since the party launched its reforms. "The folk festivals show that we are trying to bring the country back to the roots of our traditional culture and customs," says Vu Quang, who heads Hanoi's Religious Affairs Committee.

The Chu Dong Tu festival cost more than Dong 100 million (US$9,500), a massive sum in a country where per capita income is only around US$200 a year. But villagers insist that raising money from donations has been easier than trying to recreate the ancient ceremony.

Although many of the traditional costumes, musical instruments and other items of worship had been buried for safekeeping during the 1940s, most of these items were badly damaged over the next four decades. As a result, a group of elderly villagers began the painstaking task of trying to recreate the elaborate religious regalia from memory.

Many other traditional rural customs have also been restored since the party decided to abandon farm cooperatives and liberalise its social policies. Most villages have begun rebuilding their dinh, or communal houses, and Buddhist pagodas, many of which had been turned into granaries during agricultural collectivisation.

Weddings, which have long been treated as largely civil ceremonies, are once again being performed in front of traditional ancestor altars. Further, elaborate rites commemorating ancestors are again tolerated, and many grandmothers have resumed "adopting" their grandchildren to deities to fend off evil spirits.

Hanoi hopes festivals can bolster traditional values.

Spiritual Renewal

When in doubt, ask a fortune-teller

HANOI — Nguyen Thi Sen sits on the floor chanting Buddhist prayers in front of the Hanoi family's traditional ancestor altar — laden with fruit, glutinous rice, "555" brand cigarettes, cans of local Halida beer and burning incense. Several dozen relatives with their hands clasped in prayer sit behind the medium as she calls up the departed spirit of Nguyen Van Tuc, who had died 30 years earlier.

More than an hour after the ceremony began, Tuc's spirit suddenly "enters" Sen's body. The medium at first gently rubs the head of Tuc's former wife, now in her 80s, and whispers softly to the deceased man's daughters and grandchildren. Moments later, Sen begins talking loudly, smoking three cigarettes at a time and taking gulps of fiery rice alcohol.

Tuc's daughter, Nguyen Thanh Mai, a school teacher in Hanoi, asks the spirit about the future of her marriage. "Your husband is having an affair, but he won't divorce you," the spirit says. "But to keep your husband, you should stop quarrelling with him, particularly when he comes home late at night and only gives you a little money."

Tuc's spirit also has advice for Mai on how to cure her advanced case of breast cancer. He tells her to drink a cup of water from the ancestral altar and a glass of rice alcohol every day for nine days. The spirit also recommends that Mai burn a paper image of herself and to put a red paper amulet, which Sen gives Mai, under her pillow each night for the next nine days.

Sen is a 38-year-old mother of seven who runs a bustling fortune-telling and faith-healing enterprise out of a temple in her house in the northern port city of Haiphong. She has not always been as open about her livelihood as she is today. After the Communist Party ousted the French colonial power in 1954, the country's zealous new rulers launched a campaign to stamp out fortune-telling, faith-healing, communicating with the dead and other "superstitious" practices.

When Sen began fortune-telling 12 years ago, local officials destroyed her temple, she says. But since the party mounted economic reforms and began loosening its rigorous social controls in the late 1980s, many of these long-repressed practices have returned with a vengeance.

Sen now accepts invitations from all over northern Vietnam, and has so many visitors that she has had to open a guesthouse to accommodate them all. "Police and government investigators still sometimes visit me, but they no longer do anything," she says. That indicates the government, at least on paper, still considers her activities to be illegal.

Even in the capital of communist Vietnam, few people make any major decisions without consulting a fortune-teller. In the past two years, fortune-tellers have resumed their activities on almost every city block, though many of them still operate behind other business "fronts." Tran Van Vinh, a popular 87-year-old fortune-teller in Hanoi's suburbs who learned his skills from his father and grandfather, says more than 10 people visit him each day.

Young people come seeking his advice about which day they should get married and whether they will be happy with their proposed partner. Others want him to check his traditional almanac to determine when to begin building a house, launch a new business venture or bury their deceased relatives.

Do Vietnam's communist leaders ever come seeking suggestions about which day to hold an important meeting or travel abroad? "High-ranking officials never come saying they're officials," Vinh says. "But they ask their children or wives to come secretly."

One Hanoi official admits that he consults fortune-tellers before making major decisions, even though he does not believe in them. The party member says he follows their advice so his colleagues, relatives and friends will not be able to admonish him if things go wrong.

All in
The Family

One thing is booming: the population

HANOI — Nguyen Sy Nham and his wife, Nguyen Thi Nhung, are helping to dispel the government's dream of doubling Vietnam's living standards by 2000. Despite official pleas that couples have only two children, Nhung gave birth to their 10th child.

"I didn't want so many children, but I didn't know how to avoid it," Nham says. Ironically, his village of Khuong Dinh is located in the suburbs of Hanoi, only six kilometres from the headquarters of the National Committee for Population and Family Planning. "My wife was fitted with an intra-uterine device three or four times, but she had a negative reaction, so it had to be removed," says the farmer, who is struggling to support his family by raising rice and vegetables on a 360-square-metre plot of land.

But problems with intra-uterine devices and lack of knowledge about how to avoid pregnancies are only two causes of Vietnam's exploding population. Other important factors are the strong Confucian preference to have boys to carry on the family name and the desire by farmers to have a large number of workers, says Mai Ky, the minister in charge of population and family planning. A programme to curb the people boom is one key area where foreign aid can go a long way.

The population growth rate of 2.2% annually makes Vietnam the world's seventh-fastest-growing nation. At this rate, the population, estimated at 71 million by the end of 1992, will exceed 80 million by 2000.

Alarmed by this prospect, the ruling Communist Party

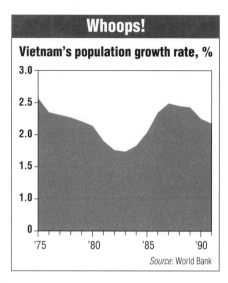

Whoops!

Vietnam's population growth rate, %

Source: World Bank

Central Committee in January passed a resolution warning that the country faced disaster unless further steps were taken to rein in population growth. It increased by 250% Ky's 1993 budget to promote family planning, but he still receives only 10 US cents per capita. Many neighbouring countries spend roughly six times that.

In the late 1980s, only 38% of the couples in child-bearing years used modern contraceptives, and four-fifths of these used intra-uterine devices. Only 1% used condoms and 0.9% used birth-control pills. To help the country expand the production of contraceptives, the UN Population Fund provided US$4 million to build a condom factory in Ho Chi Minh City in 1989 and has begun supplying pills.

Overall, the UN fund is providing US$25 million to Vietnam in 1992-95, its third-largest budget after China and India. The government is also talking to the Asian Development Bank about lending Vietnam money to provide credits to families who follow the government's exhortations to have no more than two children.

Despite years of war and international isolation, Vietnam has made considerable progress in family planning, particularly in urban areas. According to the country's 1989 census, the fertility rate for women aged 15 to 49 fell to 3.8 births per woman in 1985-88, down from a rate of 4.7 in 1980-84. Ky says the government hopes to reduce the annual population growth to 1.7% by the year 2000.

"The target is attainable, but only if foreign aid to expand the availability of contraceptives is forthcoming," says Anil Deolalikar, a consultant to the World Bank.

Even War Heroes Cry

Veterans dismayed by daring antiwar novel

HANOI — *The Sorrow of War*, a novel about a young soldier's loss of innocence during Vietnam's war with the US, was bound to create a literary and political storm.

The novel verges on heresy in a country that has turned the war into a sacred nationalist struggle and the mainstay of the Communist Party's legitimacy. It marks the first challenge to the party's glorification of the conflict by none other than a combat veteran-turned-author. And to complicate matters, the Vietnam Writers Association named it one of the best three novels of 1991.

After the award was announced in September 1991, letters of protest began flooding the Writers Association. Army veterans and literary critics condemned both the novel and the award. And in this potent mix of art and politics, *The Sorrow of War* raises questions about the very content of nationalism in Vietnam.

The Sorrow of War was written by 40-year-old Bao Ninh, who fought in some of the Revolutionary Army's fiercest battles in the central highlands and in Cambodia. He has all the markings of a revolutionary hero, including being twice injured; his credentials make his novel of the war all the more threatening to the powers that be.

The war's horrors unfold in *The Sorrow of War* through the experiences of a young soldier, who is convinced he is participating in a "holy" campaign for national liberation. As he goes off to fight, he leaves behind a girlfriend who tried to stop him from joining the army.

But by the time he returns from the battlefield, this once-idealistic soldier has become a deeply troubled man, tormented by the death of so many of his friends and unable to adapt to civilian life. His bewildered girlfriend breaks off their relationship.

Although scores of novels have been written since the war ended in 1975, most of them were penned by political officers who participated in little actual combat. But Bao Ninh's highly decorated division launched the March 1975 attack on Boun Ma Thuot (formerly Ban Me Thuot), which marked the beginning of Hanoi's final offensive to topple the US-backed government in South Vietnam. Six weeks later Saigon's Tan Son Nhut Airport was captured, ending the war.

"I wrote this novel because most other books about the war are inadequate," asserts Ninh. "I'm angry about these novels because they only advertise about the war," he says, suggesting that most writers ignore the ghastliness of death and focus instead on the bravery of soldiers and camaraderie among fighters.

Many veterans and literary critics argue, however, that Ninh exaggerates the horrors of the battlefield. "The view of the soldier in this novel is so dark and utterly tragic," Maj.-Gen. Ho Phuong wrote in *Van Nghe*, the Writers Association weekly. "It seems he only sees death and miserable things."

Much of the novel's controversy centres on one sentence that challenges an underlying theme of history as told by the party: Vietnam's repeated wars against foreign invaders are the most glorious pages in the country's past. "If Vietnam has another war," the novel's main character declares, "let another person provide the shoulder."

But Ninh's novel is unrelenting for it also depicts the disillusionment of many fighters since the war ended. "Most soldiers thought they were struggling for social equality, democracy, liberty and national reconstruction," he says. "But after 16 years few things in this beautiful picture have been realised . . . most real soldiers are unhappy and disappointed."

After the war ended, Ninh turned down the army's invitation to begin officer training, hoping finally to put the war behind him. But he has found that almost impossible. "When I look to the right and to the left, I always see the war," he says.

Ninh believes the time has come for Vietnam to re-evaluate the country's victory over the Americans, using criteria other than the victory of the party. "Our political leaders need to reassess the war in terms of its impact on ordinary Vietnamese, who sacrificed a great number of children and lost a lot of blood," he says.

Help or Hindrance?

Investors find opportunities — and troubles

HO CHI MINH CITY — Britain's Tootal Group belongs to an elite breed among foreign investors in Vietnam.

Quick to take advantage of the swing towards market-oriented economics, its executives arrived in Ho Chi Minh City in 1988. Within a relatively short time, they had signed up a local partner to produce sewing thread, obtained a 10-year exemption from profits tax and invested US$750,000 in machinery for a plant in the eastern suburbs of the city.

The factory began operating in 1990, producing 120 tonnes of spun polyester thread for Vietnam's growing garment industry. In 1992, it produced 240 tonnes — a quarter of it for export.

Tootal's experience shows that fruitful investment opportunities exist in Vietnam for foreign companies with modest expectations. Yet the company's comparatively painless entry stands in sharp contrast to that of thousands of others.

Many of the investors who have stampeded towards the country since it sought foreign capital in 1987 have run headlong into stifling bureaucracy, incompetent or greedy officials and frequent regulation changes. Investment approvals are soaring, but most of the foreign money that has actually been spent has gone into oil exploration or hotel projects, both of which can be viewed as special cases. Licences granted to manufacturing projects have begun to rise sharply, but actual disbursements in industrial projects have been slow to take off.

Hanoi's foreign-investment code, introduced in late 1987,

is one of Asia's most liberal. Foreign companies are allowed 100% ownership, or up to 99% equity in joint ventures (the approach Hanoi prefers). Tax breaks are provided for projects that generate exports, employment, hard-currency earnings or technology transfers. Projects that harness Vietnam's abundant natural resources also receive tax breaks.

The country also has made great strides in reforming its banking system. But foreign businessmen suggest that Vietnam still has much to do if it is to jump-start its economy out of the near-bankruptcy left by war and socialist mismanagement.

Some of the obstacles cannot be removed by decree. The foremost are ideological resistance to business — Vietnam remains a communist state — and international isolation. The US embargo imposed after Vietnam's 1978 invasion of Cambodia continues to deter aid and investment. However, the US announced on 2 July 1993 that it will no longer oppose loans from such agencies as the International Monetary Fund (IMF) and the World Bank.

Vietnam has some powerful lures for foreign investors — among them coal, rubber, coffee and rice; prospects for oil; a cheap, disciplined labour force; and a potential consumer market of nearly 71 million people.

Investment approvals have increased sharply since the beginning of 1991. That year's US$1.1 billion was double the total for 1990, while approvals in the first nine months of 1992 equalled the value for all of 1991. The average size of projects also has increased, to more than US$10 million from only US$1 million in 1988-89.

The latest rush brings the amount of investment approved between mid-1988 and the end of 1992 to 555 projects with a total capital of US$4.6 billion. Of this, roughly US$1.2 billion had been disbursed by the end of 1992, according to the State Committee for Cooperation and Investment (SCCI). The lion's share has been spent by foreign oil companies, which have signed 23 contracts to look for offshore oil and by investors in hotels, who are seeking to cash in on the country's sizeable tourist potential.

For Hanoi, an encouraging sign is that a higher proportion of the recent licences have been for projects in industry. But 90% of these projects involve capital of less than US$10 million and only two are worth more than US$100 million. Vietnamese officials are disappointed that less than 7% of the foreign capital has been pledged to the key sectors of agriculture, forestry and fisheries.

Few foreign companies have invested in developing the country's backward infrastructure, except for two large satellite earth stations installed by Australia's Overseas Telecommunications International (OTCI). Mining also has received little foreign investment so far, at least in part because of Hanoi's delays in granting licences for this sector.

By the end of 1992, the licences for 86 projects worth US$520.7 million had been cancelled by SCCI or had been dissolved ahead of schedule.

"People who come with low expectations and fairly low technology can succeed," says a foreign banker in Ho Chi Minh City who monitors investment activity. "The jury is still out on high-profile investments. These need a lead time of two to three years, so they're only starting their activities."

Excluding oil and gas projects, over 45% of the projects — worth US$1.6 billion — have been granted for ventures in Ho Chi Minh City, in the heart of the former capitalist south. Most of the others are located in the fertile Mekong delta or along the coast — avoiding, to some extent, the problems of poor internal transport. Only 10% of Vietnam's roads are surfaced, and even many of these are in serious disrepair. More than half its bridges are temporary structures, while at least 50 major river crossings are served only by ferries or pontoons.

Three-quarters of all licensed projects are joint ventures. Officials often steer foreign companies away from production-sharing or 100% ownership, even though these are permitted by the investment code. Do Hoang Phu, general director of the Commerce Ministry's Foreign Investment Department, says investors usually realise they need a Vietnamese partner to gain knowledge of local procedures and the legal

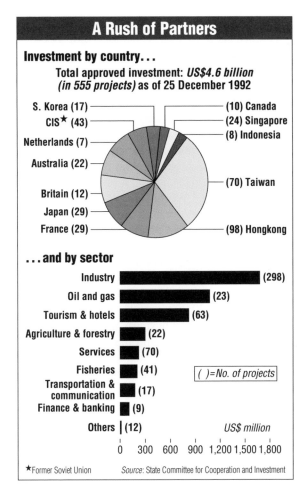

A Rush of Partners

Investment by country...

Total approved investment: *US$4.6 billion
(in 555 projects)* **as of 25 December 1992**

S. Korea (17)
CIS★ (43)
Netherlands (7)
Australia (22)
Britain (12)
Japan (29)
France (29)

(10) Canada
(24) Singapore
(8) Indonesia
(70) Taiwan
(98) Hongkong

...and by sector

Industry (298)
Oil and gas (23)
Tourism & hotels (63)
Agriculture & forestry (22)
Services (70)
Fisheries (41)
Transportation & communication (17)
Finance & banking (9)
Others (12)

( ) = No. of projects

US$ million

0   300   600   900   1,200 1,500 1,800

★ Former Soviet Union   *Source*: State Committee for Cooperation and Investment

system.

Taiwan has emerged as Vietnam's largest foreign investor; many Taiwanese are putting together projects with ethnic Chinese relatives or friends in Ho Chi Minh City. Hongkong has the largest number of projects, but ranks second in approved investment.

Japan, which already had become Vietnam's second-largest trading partner following the collapse of the Soviet Union, dramatically stepped up its investment in late 1992, when Tokyo resumed its assistance to Hanoi. Until Tokyo began granting concessionary credits to Vietnam, Japanese companies had been wary about investing, largely out of fear of retaliation by the US.

Washington insists it will maintain its trade embargo until Hanoi accounts for US servicemen still missing from the Vietnam War. Even so, President George Bush eased US sanctions in 1992 in response to increased Vietnamese cooperation in resolving the problem. And President Bill Clinton maintained the embargo even as he removed US obstacles to loans from the IMF and World Bank.

The largest Western investors are France, Britain, Australia, the Netherlands and Canada, which have companies involved in oil exploration. Overseas Vietnamese — who fled the country after the communist victory in 1975 and settled in the West — received 16 licences in 1990 to invest US$26 million. But these figures fell to only three licences worth less than US$500,000 in 1991.

Despite growing foreign business interest in the country, Vietnamese officials readily admit that investing in Vietnam is difficult. "We haven't yet created a good environment for foreign investors," says Phu, acknowledging weaknesses in infrastructure, services and the legal system.

Since promulgating the foreign investment law in 1987, the government has introduced more than 90 laws and decrees on such subjects as technology transfer, banking, labour, land and income tax. More ordinances are on the drawing board.

In late 1992, Vietnam's National Assembly approved sweeping amendments to the foreign investment law, granting new tax concessions to foreign investors and allowing private Vietnamese firms to form joint ventures with foreign companies. The assembly also agreed to extend the duration of joint ventures to 50 years — and "in necessary cases" to 70 years — from 20 years.

But large gaps remain in the legal system. There is a shortage of lawyers, and Vietnam still has no laws governing bankruptcy. The question of how commercial disputes will be resolved is still far from clear. "What if we have a dispute and say we want arbitration in Geneva?" an oil-company executive asks. "They'll just laugh."

Even where laws exist, foreign companies often face different interpretations from different state agencies. Moreover, regulations are prone to change with little notice.

Some of the harshest criticisms are reserved for the country's cumbersome bureaucracy. Complaints range from simple inefficiency to jurisdictional disputes among officials and organisations keen to expand their influence or reap some other advantage. "The main difficulty is competition between the local and central government, because there's a lot of money to be made on an investment project," a banker says. He adds that the police, too, are eager to inspect contracts "not only to control foreigners but to make business themselves."

In an attempt to overcome this jousting and present a coherent set of policies, Hanoi in mid-1989 set up the SCCI to approve investment applications and act as a go-between for foreign companies and the government. The committee has ministerial-level status. Its head, Dau Ngoc Xuan, is a member of the Communist Party Central Committee.

As a newcomer, however, the SCCI is still a relatively weak player in Vietnamese politics. It does not have exclusive responsibility to interpret foreign-investment provisions. All but the smallest, simplest projects are sent for scrutiny or approval by the Council of Ministers, which includes the heads of all government ministries and commissions.

Foreign investors also suspect that not all officials are equally enthusiastic about an invasion of foreign capitalists. A hotel manager says his company was viewed initially by some government officials as an "imperialist" influence. Even former party chief Nguyen Van Linh, the architect of Vietnam's open-door policy, who stepped down in 1991, occasionally expressed reservations about the potentially negative impact of foreign investment. "When one opens the door, dust and flies also come in," he once observed.

In addition, Vietnam's financial system is badly under-developed. A desperate shortage of hard currency makes it almost impossible for a potential investor to obtain credit locally. And Vietnamese partners find it difficult to obtain local-currency financing because the government curtails credit in an attempt to hold back inflation.

One exception has been the project to refurbish Hanoi's Thong Nhat Hotel, a joint venture between several French and Vietnamese partners, which received a US$2 million loan from two Vietnamese banks. But approval even for this relatively small amount took nearly one year.

Loans from foreign banks are also hard to arrange because most of them are still nervous about investing in Vietnam. In addition, Hanoi bars joint ventures from opening offshore accounts except in "special cases," which makes it difficult for borrowers to put up collateral on a bank loan.

The few exceptions to this ruling include Australian telecom concern OTCI, which was given permission to collect its international phone charges in an offshore account, and the Thong Nhat Hotel, which was allowed to set up a foreign account to repay a US$5.3 million loan from a consortium of four French banks.

The lack of credit means foreign investors must depend on their own capital for finance. Vietnamese officials hope more funding soon will be available locally since foreign banks began opening branches in Vietnam in 1992. But foreign bankers predict that Hanoi will be disappointed. "This won't change the basic problem that Vietnam is still a big risk," one says.

Vietnam's lack of hard currency limits foreign investors to projects that generate their own foreign exchange. This prevents ventures from producing only for the domestic market, despite its sizeable potential, because the foreign partners will be unable to obtain hard currency to repatriate their profits or to import new equipment.

Another source of difficulty is that Vietnam is not nearly as cheap a place to operate in as Hanoi claims. Government labour policies require foreign companies to hire workers through a service organisation and pay a minimum wage of US$35 a month, theoretically at least. This rate was reduced in early 1992 from US$50 a month because of protests from foreign investors.

The workers themselves often take home only about 30% of their income. "We find Vietnamese cost more than their counterparts in Malaysia or Indonesia, but they are receiving less," says an oil official.

Other operating costs also are steep. Recently the government began charging foreign-investment projects higher rates for electricity and water — and the charges must be paid in US dollars.

Furthermore, Ho Chi Minh City suffers up to four days of power cuts each week during the first half of the year because of the low water level at the Soviet-built Tri An dam, forcing many companies to install generators. The manager of a Taiwanese joint-venture shoe factory says this costs him an additional US$200 a day in fuel costs alone.

Companies depending on international communications are also hard-hit. "Our telecommunications charges are more than double the cost of all our other operating expenses," says one businessman. "In Singapore, they're only 2% of our total costs."

Similar kinds of concerns have created difficulties for Tootal's thread venture, despite its early success in achieving volume production. The partners have lobbied the government — so far without success — to change a tax structure that imposes a 4% levy on revenue because the company produces for the local market. Companies producing exclusively for export are not taxed.

The Tootal venture nevertheless stands as a benchmark of the kind of manufacturing project that Vietnam needs to attract. Chief among the ingredients of its success: its local partner, Phong Phu Textile Mill, was an established company that exports cotton fabrics and garments.

Many of Phong Phu's executives and engineers were familiar with Western business practices, having worked for the company before South Vietnam fell to the communists in

1975. Deputy manager Khieu Thien Thuat, who was appointed to head the joint venture, had studied textiles and management in France.

Tootal also has succeeded because it hit on a product for which there is growing demand within Vietnam. Thuat sees garment-making as an expanding industry, noting that at least 40 companies from Hongkong, Taiwan, Japan, Germany, Thailand and Malaysia have signed agreements to set up garment ventures.

Obstacle Course

Foreigners complain of red-tape and meddling

HO CHI MINH CITY — Investment in Vietnam is not for the faint-hearted, impatient or those looking to make a quick buck. Successful investment, according to foreign businessmen, requires persistence and, crucially, a competent and well-intentioned Vietnamese partner who can fight through the bureaucratic maze.

Robert Verschoyle, an Irishman who established himself in Ho Chi Minh City in 1989, learned several of these lessons while scouting opportunities for a former employer, Industrial Marketing Group (IMG), a British holding company.

Verschoyle says IMG, which earlier had been involved in selling computers to the former Soviet Union and Eastern Europe, saw Vietnam as a potential new market. His research, however, suggested it was too early to try to market hi-tech goods in Vietnam. Instead, IMG elected to go for an entirely different venture.

The company invested US$250,000 to set up an export-oriented timber-processing business in Thu Duc, a suburb of Ho Chi Minh City. It also signed a business-cooperation contract with Nhatico, a construction corporation run by the city government, under which Nhatico was to obtain the necessary operating licences and supply timber to IMG.

Nine months later, Nhatico still had not obtained a licence, even though the State Committee for Cooperation and Investment (SCCI) had pledged to rule on foreign applications within three months. As Verschoyle grew more impatient, relations between the two partners soured. They broke down completely when IMG rejected a 370-cubic-metre shipment of timber blighted by "blue stain," a condition caused by failure to treat pine logs quickly after felling.

Nhatico retaliated by getting local officials to block another IMG timber load that was due to leave by ship the next day. By the time IMG had succeeded in reversing the blocking order, the ship had sailed. "We had 1,000 cubic metres of timber sitting around, which knocked our cash flow on the head. We had to wait a month and a half for the next ship," Verschoyle recalls.

In retrospect, Verschoyle admits to some missteps, including importing equipment before he was granted authorisation to operate. "We thought our idea would be snatched up by the government because it was an 'aid' programme," he says, referring to IMG's agreement to pay its suppliers on delivery, rather than after the timber had been processed or sold.

But he also accuses Nhatico of hidden motives, believing the Vietnamese side hoped IMG would become fed up waiting for a licence and would withdraw, leaving behind its equipment and buildings.

Verschoyle says IMG probably will suspend its timber business until it finds another partner, but he does not expect IMG to leave Vietnam; the long-term prospects are still bright, he believes. While awaiting a change of fortune, he has gone back to rebuilding a 72-foot yacht he recently bought in Haiphong.

Other businessmen also have their tales of frustration. Among their complaints:

▶ **Red tape**. "The downside of doing business is the length of time it takes to get anything done," says Clive Fairfield, co-owner of Singapore-based Continental Offshore, which mostly trades but has also invested in several small sawmills and garment factories in Vietnam.

"There's a lot of collective irresponsibility — nobody seems to be in a position to make a decision," Fairfield adds, though he notes: "The plus of working here is that many Vietnamese are trying hard to make [your venture] work,

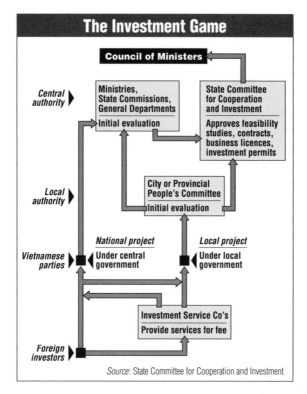

The Investment Game

Source: State Committee for Cooperation and Investment

despite the system." Indeed, Vietnamese staff are generally praised by foreign businessmen as being hard workers and adaptable.

Taiwan investor C. F. Chang, chairman of the Pan Viet Corp., also reports difficulties with obstructionist local bureaucrats. In addition to being involved in several joint-venture housing projects, the company is setting up plantations to grow bananas for export. But it stopped work on a US$2 million banana-research station because of constant interference from local officials. "All they wanted to know was when they would get their money . . . they don't understand that agricultural projects need long-term investment," he says.

▶ **Internal conflicts**. When the Saigon Star Hotel opened in Ho Chi Minh City in 1991, it obtained a permit from the city traffic department to allow guests to park their cars on the street. A few days later, the district police declared the permit invalid. Hotel manager Billy Or, one of four Hongkong-based partners in the project, suggested the police talk to the Vietnamese side of the joint venture — the Ministry of Defence. Street parking was allowed.

▶ **Customs procedures**. "My biggest problems come when I suddenly have to change an order," says another Taiwan businessman, James Huang, manager of Lac Ty, a joint venture producing canvas shoes for export to Europe. "I can't know in March what type of shoes my customers will order in June. But changing a shipment can take months, while I have to explain why I want to change the materials I'm importing."

Others, however, have found the Vietnamese customs service to be highly efficient. "I've never had a container waiting more than two days," says Continental's Fairfield. "If you get your paperwork correct, no one gives a damn."

▶ **Corruption**. The country's poorly paid customs officials are likely to speed up their procedures if offered some reward. "Fifty-thousand dong [roughly US$5] here, a hundred thousand there, a bottle someplace else — it's the same everywhere in the world," says one foreign businessman.

Some foreigners, however, complain that corruption is becoming so widespread, particularly in dealing with certain state offices, that it is no longer possible to work above board. The results can be perverse. "If I offer US$150 for a cubic metre of timber and no backhander, the guy who offers US$100 plus a US$5 backhander will get the contract," a source says. "Many managers are only interested in feathering their own nest and are quite happy to operate their state company at a loss."

Yet Pan Viet's Chang declares: "We're big investors in Vietnam, and until now, I didn't pay a cent under the table."

Wooing Them Home

Overseas Vietnamese hesitate to invest

HO CHI MINH CITY — Thirteen years after he fled Vietnam in the wake of the communist victory in 1975, Tran Van Phu returned in search of business opportunities. Armed with a degree in business management, a French passport and money he had made in Paris, Phu invested US$90,000 to set up Scavi Vietnam, a small factory producing women's underwear in the suburbs of Ho Chi Minh City.

Phu hired 100 workers, including his sister, who manages the factory, four brothers and their spouses. Scavi expected in 1992 to export 1.5 million items of underwear to France and other European countries. Phu's target is to capture 10% of the women's underwear market in France by 1995.

Phu is optimistic about his investment experience. "Of course, it would be better if officials were more competent," he says, alluding to the bureaucrats with whom he has to deal. "But my principal target was not to make money here; it's easier to make money in France. I came to help develop the country and to help my family."

Phu's venture appears to have met the communist government's best expectations when it launched its economic reforms and began wooing Vietnamese living abroad in the late 1980s. He brought back his savings, expertise and foreign connections to help boost an economy struggling after years of stagnation brought on by socialist mismanagement and international isolation.

But many other overseas Vietnamese still hesitate in their dealings with Vietnam. Over 105,000 Vietnamese living abroad visited Ho Chi Minh City in 1992, up from less than 62,000 in 1991, according to estimates of the city's Overseas Vietnamese Committee, a quasi-governmental organisation set up to court overseas Vietnamese.

Although the number of visitors is growing, it is still only a small fraction of the estimated 2 million Vietnamese living abroad. Nearly half live in the US, while France, Canada and Australia also have large overseas Vietnamese communities.

Most of those who return come to visit their relatives, but some come looking for trade, to share their technical skills or foreign business connections. Only a handful have come to invest and the experiences of many of these have disap-

Foreign investment benefits Vietnamese workers.

pointed both Hanoi and the overseas Vietnamese investor.

Much of the caution of the overseas Vietnamese in dealing with Vietnam is related to the circumstances under which they left the country. Most fled as boat people to escape repressive policies or the country's grinding poverty after the communist victory in 1975. Some of them, particularly among the nearly 1 million who settled in the US, still harbour hopes of toppling Hanoi's communist regime.

As a result, the party's security apparatus remains distrustful of overseas Vietnamese, particularly since the unravelling of communism in Eastern Europe and the Soviet Union. *Quan Doi Nhan Dan*, the army daily, warned in late 1991 that "the imperialists are using the exiled reactionaries as shock troops to seek an alliance with [local] opposition elements to step up their peaceful evolutionary activities with a goal towards creating disturbances and riots to overthrow the socialist regime in Vietnam."

The paper charged that some overseas Vietnamese returning on visits were bringing in "huge amounts of reactionary documents, books, magazines and psychological letters with incendiary contents." In April 1991, an overseas Vietnamese doctor from the US was arrested and expelled after he allegedly was found to be carrying documents prepared by the writer Duong Thu Huong, criticising the Communist Party and its human-rights record.

Late in 1990, a Vietnamese court found a group of 37 overseas Vietnamese guilty of trying to sneak back into Vietnam with weapons in an attempt to overthrow the government.

These events make some overseas Vietnamese wary about returning. "When I first came back, I was afraid I was risking my life," says a 30-year-old, who fled in 1980 and settled in the US. "But I was surprised how much the city has changed. People are now left alone to make money.

"Sometimes I'd like to come back here to live, but I don't know what will happen in the future," he says. "In case I get in trouble and get arrested, who will get me out?" he asks, referring to the fact that the US has no embassy in Vietnam.

But the problems between the overseas Vietnamese and their homeland are more than political. Some overseas Vietnamese have created resentment by flaunting the money they made abroad and by swindling Vietnamese with less experience in international business. A store manager in Long An province, east of Ho Chi Minh City, committed suicide in 1990 when an overseas Vietnamese company failed to deliver the goods for which he had paid in advance.

"Some overseas Vietnamese come back with fancy calling cards and promise to invest millions of dollars," says one Vietnamese businessman. "But once they get a lot of money in advance from the Vietnamese side, they disappear." Others promise to supply sophisticated equipment and then import used goods, charging several times the real price, he says.

Overseas Vietnamese are also blamed for contributing to some of the country's social problems. "Many of the sex scandals in Ho Chi Minh City involve overseas Vietnamese," a journalist says. When a woman in the city in 1990 became the first person to test positive for AIDS, the state-run press attributed it to her sexual relations with two overseas Vietnamese.

Nevertheless, some Vietnamese women believe overseas Vietnamese men make good husbands because they offer an easy ticket out of the country. One young Ho Chi Minh City resident says some of his friends pretend to be overseas Vietnamese because they find it easier to get women to go out with them.

"There are as many different kinds of overseas Vietnamese as there are fingers on your hand," says a local businessman working in a joint venture with an overseas Vietnamese from the US. "Some cheat, but many want to do serious business."

Overseas Vietnamese companies played a key role in opening up Vietnam's economy in the early 1980s. They began trading with Vietnam when the country was still largely closed, except for its relations with the Soviet Union and Eastern Europe.

The estimated 60 overseas Vietnamese companies licensed to operate in Ho Chi Minh City imported US$63 million of commodities in 1990, while exporting US$19 million of seafood, agricultural products, art and handicraft items.

A more important contribution to the struggling economy is the millions of dollars overseas Vietnamese send or smuggle to their relatives, particularly in Ho Chi Minh City, which has 250,000 households with family members living abroad. Vietnamese economists estimate that Vietnamese abroad sent cash and gold worth at least US$500 million to their families in Vietnam in 1992. This equals roughly one-fifth of Vietnam's export earnings that year.

Overseas Vietnamese also have contributed technical know-how to their native land. Vietnam was long isolated from technological and scientific advances in the rest of the world due to the economic sanctions imposed on Hanoi following its 1978 invasion of Cambodia. Many returning Vietnamese professionals who come to visit their families spend some of their time giving lectures or holding seminars on economics, medicine or law.

Overseas Vietnamese played a key role in bringing computer technology to Vietnam in the late 1980s. A few years ago, a group of Vietnamese in Germany introduced the Liksin general printing house to advances in the printing industry, though company officials complain that they were overcharged for some of the equipment they bought. Another group of Vietnamese from France helped set up a heart-treatment centre in Ho Chi Minh City.

"The strength of the overseas Vietnamese is not in economics, but in the intellectual field," says U Thi Anh, vice president of the city's Overseas Vietnamese Committee. She is referring to the fact that Vietnamese have traditionally been less interested in business than in such fields as scientific research, teaching and medicine. "We need to exploit this aspect more," she says.

Some overseas Vietnamese play an important role as brokers between Vietnam and foreign investors, who committed US$4.6 billion in the five years after Hanoi introduced its foreign investment law in late 1987. Some large foreign firms retain overseas Vietnamese consultants to help deal with officials often inexperienced in international commerce or to break through Hanoi's maddening bureaucracy and vague and often-changing regulations. Others hire Vietnamese living abroad to run their investment projects in Vietnam.

But investment by overseas Vietnamese themselves has been small and appears to be slowing down rather than growing. Since 1988, they have been granted only 23 investment licences worth US$38 million in fields such as processing agricultural products and seafood, assembling electronic equipment, repairing hotels and setting up service companies, according to Hanoi's State Committee for Cooperation and Investment (SCCI).

In 1991 and 1992, when investment by foreign companies increased sharply, overseas Vietnamese were granted only two licences to invest US$835,000.

Ten overseas Vietnamese projects, worth US$8.1 million, have expired or have had their licences withdrawn by SCCI. "Many of the overseas Vietnamese who invest lack capital and their technical know-how is not very good," says Phan Huu Thang, the deputy manager of SCCI in Hanoi.

Some Vietnamese economists believe investment by overseas Vietnamese will pick up only after Washington lifts its economic embargo. "Many overseas Vietnamese in the US have accumulated a lot of money," one economist says. "It's not a lot of money in the US, but it's good for doing business in Vietnam. With access to the American market, the overseas Vietnamese can make good business here."

But at least some overseas Vietnamese attribute their reluctance to invest to more than their lack of capital or American policy. Many who came back to invest have been disillusioned by the country's inept bureaucrats, corruption, suspicion by the country's security apparatus, and what they consider to be the Communist Party's half-hearted steps towards a real free-market economy.

Some become so disheartened that they leave Vietnam a second time. Take the case of Tuan, who gave up his job as a computer specialist in Canada in 1990 to return to Vietnam to set up a service company for a foreign investor. Tuan served as an officer in the US-backed South Vietnamese army, but left the country to study abroad shortly before the communist victory in 1975. "Vietnam has so many problems, so I came back wanting to help," he says.

But Tuan faced troubles right from the start. It took him three months just to get authorisation to open an escrow account and two months to be given a competent accountant so that the company could begin operating.

When he finally opened for business, Tuan, who requests that his real name and that of his company not be used, says he quickly wooed away 25 customers from a competing state-owned company, because his rates were lower and his service more prompt. But his success was short-lived. One by one his clients pulled out, letting him know that they had come under pressure to use the state-owned competitor.

Then a few months later, Tuan was attacked in a local press article that used confidential business information known only to the city's People's Committee and a state-owned bank. He concluded that he was caught in a plot by the state sector to get rid of a potential competitor.

Tuan faced personal frustrations as well. As an overseas Vietnamese, he got only three-month visas, though the foreign investment code promises investors one-year permits. He also had to get police approval every time he wanted to take his children to the beach resort of Vung Tau, 100 km southeast of the city.

"If they want overseas Vietnamese to invest, they have to trust us," he says. "My conclusion is that you have to be very careful about investing in Vietnam." Tuan closed his company at the end of 1991 and returned to Canada.

Thang of the SCCI says the government will have to introduce more favourable investment privileges for overseas Vietnamese if it hopes to attract more serious investment from them. The foreign investment law promulgated in 1987 promised incentives for overseas Vietnamese investors, but these have not yet been drafted. The government has promised to cut the waiting time for visas for overseas Vietnamese with foreign passports to seven days from 15.

Market Test

Ethnic Chinese re-emerge to start businesses

HO CHI MINH CITY — The construction of the new five-storey An Dong market in Cholon, the Chinatown of Ho Chi Minh City, may well symbolise the re-emergence of the ethnic Chinese as a powerful force in Vietnam's economy.

The new US$5 million market marks the first sizeable investment project in the city by a group of ethnic Chinese businessmen, who were forced out of business by the zealous Communist Party following its victory over the US-backed capitalist South Vietnam in mid-1975.

"Five years ago, no capitalist would have dared to do this," says Pham Xuan Bien, an expert on Vietnam's ethnic Chinese at the city's Institute of Social Sciences. "Now you can see the ethnic Chinese daring to start something." He attributes the change to the party's 1986 decision to move towards a free market, which means allowing the ethnic Chinese a larger role in the country's economy.

City officials had planned to rebuild the deteriorating, overcrowded old market with investment from a Singapore company, but when these plans fell through some local *hoa*, or ethnic Chinese, businessmen stepped in. La Cong Nguyen, who resumed his business activities a few years after losing three factories in 1975, called on his Chinese friends to help set up a shareholding company, the Viet-Hoa Construction Co., to build the new market.

"Our main goal is to support economic renovation," Nguyen says about the market. "Through this investment, we want to send a message to the state. If it has correct policies and uses people well, we can do big development projects."

Before the communist victory in 1975, Nguyen had operated three factories, producing sewing machines, furniture and garments for export. When the new communist government cut most of its links with the capitalist world, Nguyen was unable to market his products, prompting him to give his factories to the state. An abrupt currency change a year later left the once-wealthy businessman penniless and forced him to survive by making keys, he says.

As the party began loosening its once-doctrinaire socialist policies, Nguyen sold his furniture to raise money to begin producing animal feed, raising chickens and making noodles. Later he became a shareholder in a company exporting handicrafts and processed wood for furniture. As his business activities grew, he earned enough money to invest in the An Dong market.

Nguyen is not the only one testing the party's new policies. Thousands of other ethnic Chinese have resumed trading activities in the past few years, or have established small-scale industries processing food, producing textiles and shoes, or assembling electronic equipment.

Cholon's ethnic Chinese now control at least two-thirds of the small-scale industrial sector and one-third of the commercial activities in Ho Chi Minh City, even though they comprise only about 10% of the city's population, estimates Tran Khanh, another expert on Vietnam's ethnic Chinese at Hanoi's Southeast Institute.

According to a 1989 census, Vietnam has some 960,000 ethnic Chinese, of whom about 80% live in the south. Ho Chi Minh City, the former Saigon, had nearly 380,000 Chinese at the time of the census. The capital Hanoi had less than 10,000 — down from about 34,000 a decade earlier.

Many observers think the ethnic Chinese are still holding back in their business activities. "So far, the ethnic Chinese have put only 10-20% of their capital on the table," says Huynh Buu Son, the deputy managing director of the Saigon Bank for Industry and Trade, which is located in the heart of Cholon.

Before 1975, the ethnic Chinese had dominated South Vietnam's economy. They controlled 80% of its industry, 50% of the banking and finance, nine-tenths of the wholesale trade, half of the retail business and most of the rice trade, according to estimates by Vietnamese academics.

Most of the ethnic Chinese in what was then called Saigon lived in separate communities — the majority lived in Cholon — where they operated their own hospitals, ran their own schools using a curriculum from Taiwan, worshipped in their own temples and buried their dead in their own graveyards.

Many of these activities came to an abrupt halt after 1975, when the new communist government took over all private schools and hospitals, and began closing private companies. The last surviving businesses were shut down on the night of 24 March 1978, when the government launched its "socialist transformation" campaign and sent policemen and youth volunteers to take over the last vestiges of private industry and trade.

This move, which hit ethnic Chinese in the south hardest, prompted tens of thousands to join the boat-people exodus. China, increasingly angered by Hanoi's alliance with the Soviet Union, sharply denounced Vietnam for mistreating its Overseas Chinese residents.

As Sino-Vietnamese hostilities escalated, Hanoi became increasingly suspicious of the ethnic Chinese in the north — most of whom had supported the party's struggle against the US — and forced many to choose between moving to remote "new economic zones" and leaving for China. Many of those who stayed were stripped of their party membership, lost their army or police jobs, and saw their children barred from attending universities.

Three years after China's brief attack on Vietnam in retaliation for the Vietnamese invasion of Cambodia, Hanoi — recognising that its ethnic Chinese could play a key role in pulling the country out of its economic nosedive — began softening its stance. In 1982, the party's ruling Politburo issued a still-secret Resolution 10, which admitted that the policy of considering ethnic Chinese as "instruments of Peking reactionaries" had been a mistake.

The resolution also said the ethnic Chinese would be recognised as one of Vietnam's 54 minority groups and therefore would be regarded as Vietnamese citizens. This caused renewed anxiety among some ethnic Chinese who had retained their Taiwan passports even after the former South Vietnamese government had ordered them to take out Vietnamese citizenship.

The most dramatic change for the ethnic Chinese came in 1986, when the Communist Party's sixth congress began removing the fetters on private business. This was soon followed by moves giving the Chinese greater freedom to resume some of their former social activities and to allow them again to be involved in political life.

Ethnic Chinese were again admitted into the party and some who had lost their party memberships in the late 1970s had them restored. Today there are roughly 1,000 ethnic Chinese party members out of a nationwide total of just over 2 million, according to party officials. One ethnic Chinese member, the director of a large state-run company in Ho Chi Minh City, was elected as an alternative delegate to the seventh party congress in June 1991.

Ethnic Chinese can again serve in the army or in the Interior Ministry's security forces, and they are once again admitted to universities.

In 1988, the Ministry of Education allowed primary and secondary schools with high concentrations of ethnic Chinese students to resume teaching in Chinese, though the teachers must follow a curriculum prepared by the ministry. Ethnic Chinese have also been allowed to set up a body called the Association to Sponsor Chinese Language Teaching. "They didn't ban Chinese after 1975, but in reality they set up limitations in promoting the language," says Nguyen.

So far, no Chinese-language newspapers have reopened, although Ho Chi Minh City's official daily, *Saigon Giai Phong*, is published in Chinese. Two of the city's districts with large numbers of Chinese residents are also allowed to print local community newsletters.

The most visible change for the ethnic Chinese has been in the economy. They have returned to most of the activities in which they were involved prior to 1975 — though at a much reduced level — except for the rice-export business. Their role in the domestic rice trade is still limited, but some nationalised rice mills recently have been returned to their previous Chinese owners.

Chinese businessmen have again begun operating gold shops and are believed to play a key role in setting the city's gold prices. In 1992, the same business group that built the An Dong food market received authorisation to form the Viet Hoa (or Vietnam-China) Bank. The stockholding bank, the first operated by ethnic Chinese since 1975, opened with registered capital of Dong 20 billion (US$1.9 million).

Despite the increased business role of the ethnic Chinese, they no longer enjoy the tight monopoly in their traditional economic spheres that they did before 1975. Over a decade of discriminatory policies appear to have eliminated some of the Chinese business edge and given Vietnamese business-men time to begin competing in trading and small-scale industry.

Hanoi's policies in the late 1970s and early 1980s also appear to have partially broken up the once-resilient Chinese communities and pushed them towards increased integration with the larger Vietnamese community, according to foreign and Vietnamese observers.

The government's new policies have slowed the exodus of ethnic Chinese from Vietnam and in some cases refugees have even come back in search of new economic activities, says Bui Thanh Son, vice-chairman of Ho Chi Minh City's district 5, which includes Cholon. One Chinese businessman who had applied to join his relatives in the US under the orderly departure programme says he withdrew his application in 1989 after Hanoi's reforms started taking hold.

Although Vietnam was largely closed for a decade after 1975, many ethnic Chinese have managed to maintain close contact with Chinese communities in Taiwan, Hongkong,

Singapore and in Western countries. Bien says two-thirds of the Chinese in Ho Chi Minh City have close relatives abroad. Ethnic Chinese have found it easier to travel overseas in recent years. Since the Sino-Vietnamese border was informally reopened in the late 1980s, some have begun visiting China in search of business opportunities.

Because many Chinese businessmen lost their wealth in the late 1970s, a sizeable share of the money they are now investing comes from relatives overseas.

"People from Taiwan bring a lot of money to their relatives," says Son, the banker. Taiwan has emerged as the largest foreign investor in Vietnam, with Taiwanese firms holding licences for 70 projects worth US$1.1 billion by the end of 1992. Hongkong ranked second with a total pledged capital of US$476 million. Increasing numbers of investors from Taiwan and Hongkong are also turning to their kinsmen for help in navigating Vietnam's bureaucratic maze.

Despite increased investment by local ethnic Chinese, many are still cautious. "Most still only invest in small-scale projects with a rapid turnover," says Khanh. "If the situation isn't stable, they think they could withdraw their capital quickly."

Nguyen says many wealthier Chinese are still anxious because the government has not yet resolved the charges against them in the late 1970s. "In the past, the government said capitalists had made mistakes. What these mistakes were needs to be cleared up," he says.

Other Chinese businessmen say they are delaying larger-scale investment until they see if the party completes its moves towards a free-market economy and puts an end to many of its policies that continue to discriminate against the private sector.

"We're waiting to see the policies of the government," says Thai Thoi Tuong, who runs a workshop producing cardboard boxes for seafood exports. "I'm especially waiting to see the policy on taxes," he adds, alluding to tax policies that still give preferential treatment to state enterprises.

Line of Controversy

Power project sends warning to lenders

HANOI — Is Hanoi ready for credits from the International Monetary Fund and World Bank? Judging by need — yes. Judging by the A500 power line — perhaps not.

Designed to transfer 500 kilovolts of electricity from north to south Vietnam by means of an overland power line, the A500 project has fast become a textbook lesson on how not to impress international financial institutions.

Plagued by corruption, delays, cost overruns and inadequate planning, the 1,500-kilometre transmission line now serves as a warning to the world financial community: when access to international lending institutions is granted, Vietnam might not be equipped to handle the funds expected to pour into the country.

Warns one member of the National Assembly: "The north-south electricity line is an example of what will happen when the embargo is lifted."

Developed to ease a 25% energy shortfall in the south, the power line will draw electricity from the Soviet-built Hoa Binh hydroelectric power station southwest of Hanoi and transfer it to Ho Chi Minh City, where brownouts now reach up to four days a week during the dry season.

Difficulties with the project began almost immediately after it was launched in April 1992. The assembly, which in the past had served as little more than a rubber stamp for the Communist Party's decisions, balked when asked to approve the proposal. Its rationale: not only had construction already begun, but it had been started even before a feasibility study had been completed.

Other concerns raised by the assembly included the number of years the north will actually produce excess power to send to the south. Energy Minister Thai Phung Ne says that following the completion of the Hoa Binh power station in late 1993, the north will enjoy an electricity surplus until 1997.

But many members of the assembly's Science Committee consider that estimate too optimistic. They argue that if the US trade embargo is lifted in 1993 and foreign aid and investment subsequently increase, the north's surplus will be exhausted by 1995 — only one year after the power line is scheduled for completion. Says the same assembly member: "It would be much cheaper to buy extra turbines for the south" rather than build the trunk line.

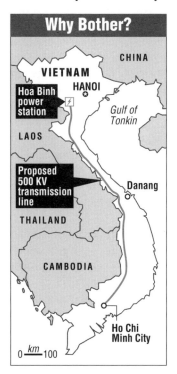

Why Bother?

CHINA

VIETNAM

HANOI

Hoa Binh power station

Gulf of Tonkin

LAOS

Proposed 500 KV transmission line

Danang

THAILAND

CAMBODIA

Ho Chi Minh City

0 —km— 100

Although the legislature eventually approved the project, some assembly members have continued to voice objections. At its December session, former speaker Le Quang Dao surprised colleagues by declaring that he had made a mistake when he pushed for approval of the line. Warning of massive cost overruns, he said the project's price tag would be at least Dong 2 trillion (US$191 million) more than the initial estimates of Dong 3 trillion. Further, he said the government had failed to listen to early objections by engineers about the project.

The power line also has its critics outside the legislature. Investors both at home and abroad have failed to show interest in the project. Minister Ne says Hanoi — which is still barred from receiving credits from international lending institutions — had hoped to finance much of the programme through concessionary credits from foreign governments and treasury bonds.

But so far, no foreign governments have offered credits and the sale of bonds has been sluggish. Four months after the bonds were issued in July 1992, Ho Chi Minh City's *Youth* magazine reported that the treasury had raised only Dong 50 billion — less than one-third of the sum targeted by the end of the year. Even worse, the magazine reported that more than 90% of that money was raised from companies that were ordered to buy the bonds.

The fact that plans for the project had not been completed before the bidding was opened to foreign suppliers has furthered the sense of disarray. Overseas firms interested in cashing in on Vietnam's first major infrastructure project since the collapse of the Soviet Union have received only a 16-page description of the project. Accustomed to being given detailed specifications from buyers, they have been forced to develop their own plans instead. They have then watched as the Vietnamese have taken those plans and used them to rewrite the actual programme. "It's difficult to put a big project together when you don't know what they want," complains one foreign bidder.

Even so, eight firms — three French, three South Korean and one each from Japan and the Ukraine — have signed contracts worth about US$280 million to supply equipment for the power line.

But in another indication that Vietnam might not be ready for the rush of projects expected in a post-embargo era, some observers have questioned whether the Vietnamese are experienced enough to construct the line without hiring a professional foreign project manager. They point out that Vietnamese contractors are building all of the towers the same height, instead of custom building each one for its specific location.

Corruption has also taken its toll on the project. The former minister of energy, Vu Ngoc Hai, was ousted in late 1992 after three of the ministry's companies were caught faking invoices claiming they had provided 4,000 tonnes of steel for the power line when only 2,300 tonnes had been delivered. "The only good thing about the project is that it provides another opportunity for people to be corrupt," charges another assembly member opposed to the A500 programme.

Despite these problems Minister Ne is convinced that the line — much of which will be built along the Ho Chi Minh Trail — will be completed by the end of 1994. He says 2,500 pole foundations, out of 3,500, were in place by late 1992, and that some of the supplies purchased from foreign companies have begun arriving.

Overwhelming though the project may seem, Hanoi's difficulties in completing the power line are not unique. Most developing countries find that their limitations often surpass their abilities to complete major infrastructure projects according to Western standards of efficiency.

But no one can fault Vietnamese ingenuity. Eighteen years after Hanoi last used the Ho Chi Minh Trail to carry soldiers and arms from the North to the South in the war against the US, it has found a new use for the route. Except this time, the government hopes that instead of military might, the power coming down the line will be a different kind — electricity.

Red Capitalists

Private enterprise flourishes despite hurdles

HANOI — Vu Duy Thai took the government seriously when it declared in 1988 that Vietnam's economy could accommodate capitalism. Although his family lost all its land in 1954 when the communists came to power in northern Vietnam, he decided to use what remained of the family fortune — 4.5 kilogrammes of gold, or about US$62,000 — to set up Hanoi's first private construction company.

In two years, Thai Thanh Construction Enterprise completed 23 building projects ranging from schools and student dormitories to shops and houses. But in December 1990, the Hanoi People's Committee drove him out of business when it required that bids for construction contracts by private companies include security deposits equivalent to the total value of the projects.

Thai, a veteran of the guerilla war against the French in the 1950s, appealed to the country's ruling Central Committee to no avail. At the end of 1991, Thai shut down his company and sold his construction equipment at a loss. He laid off more than 100 workers.

"The state says it wants equality for all economic sectors, but many officials still wish to control everything," he complains. "They have no intention to allow the establishment of private capitalists in Vietnam."

Many private businesses have failed in the past five years because of similar harassment by government officials. Difficulties obtaining credit and the country's continuing economic instability also have contributed to numerous business closures. Despite these obstacles, the private sector has begun to play a significant role in Vietnam's economy, particularly in the former capitalist south.

The private sector in Ho Chi Minh City, Vietnam's economic hub, accounted for 44% of the city's output in 1991, according to Ton Si Kinh, vice-director of the city's Institute of Economic Research. He estimates that private factories produced 51% of the city's industrial output.

The role of the private sector in trade and services is even bigger. Huynh Buu Son, deputy managing director of Saigon Bank for Industry and Trade, in Ho Chi Minh City's vibrant Chinatown, estimates that 70% of the city's trade in 1991 was controlled by private business. Even in Hanoi, long the bastion of Vietnamese communism, the private sector in the same year controlled 67% of the city's trade, services and restaurant facilities, according to the government's General Statistics Office.

Most of the estimated 350,000 private businesses that have sprung up in the past five years are small, employing less than 20-30 workers, says Nguyen Chi Vu, chairman of the Central Council of Industrial Cooperatives and Non-State Enterprises, a body set up in 1990 to help the private sector. Only a handful of private companies employ more than 1,000 workers. Less than 1,200 private companies are capitalised at more than US$20,000, Vu says.

The most successful private companies manufacture for export, which enables the owners to recoup their investment quickly. Firms producing for export also get special tax breaks. They are exempt from a revenue tax of 6-10% that is assessed against companies producing for the domestic market. An exporters' profit tax ranges from 15-25%, compared with 40% for private companies serving the domestic market.

The companies on the commanding heights of the private sector are export-oriented. Among them are: Minh Phung Factory and Huy Hoang Co., two large garment producers in Ho Chi Minh City; Binh Tien Rubber Works Corp., an ethnic Chinese firm that makes shoes in Ho Chi Minh City; and Haivinaco Ltd, which produces porcelain in Haiphong and is

Private sector drives Ho Chi Minh City's economy.

the largest private company in northern Vietnam.

"During this transition period, there are a lot of risks and also a lot of opportunities," Kinh says. "If you know how to exploit them, it is easy to get rich. But not a small number of opportunists have gone to jail." This is a reference to the head of Thanh Huong Perfume Co., who was jailed after a pyramid scheme went bust in 1990.

Adds Tang Minh Phung, managing director of the Minh Phung factory: "Many businessmen are waiting for very specific and clear policies before investing," fearful of an about-face on economic reforms. Phung is among the bold, employing 5,000 workers in a factory that exported US$20 million of garments in 1991.

Vietnam's Communist Party forced most private companies out of business after its 1975 victory against the US-backed capitalist regime in the South. Companies that survived were shut down in early 1978, when Hanoi began its socialist-transformation movement. Police and youth volunteers seized the last remnants of capitalist industry and trade in the ensuing campaign.

But the government was forced to reverse course. Social-ist mismanagement and the international isolation imposed after Vietnam's invasion of Cambodia in late 1978 brought the economy to the brink of collapse. The most dramatic changes came in 1986, when the Sixth Party Congress began lifting restrictions on private business.

By 1990, thousands of private businesses had sprung up around the country, only to go bankrupt as austerity measures to rein in hyperinflation in 1989 led to a deep recession. The collapse of hundreds of unregulated credit cooperatives in early 1990 compounded the country's economic woes.

Further, small private manufacturers that relied on mar-kets in Eastern Europe and the former Soviet Union, such as the handicraft, lacquer and rattan industries, were hard hit by the chaos facing Vietnam's former socialist allies. More re-cently, industrial production in Ho Chi Minh City has been hampered by up to four days of brownouts each week.

By mid-1991, production in the private sector had pulled out of its nosedive. After several years of falling output, the private sector grew 2.5% in 1991, according to official esti-mates. Even so, private businessmen are cautious.

"Our biggest problem is finding capital," says Bui Xuan Hai, head of Haivinaco, who was arrested in the 1980s for his business activities. "The private sector still faces dis-crimination on credit."

Indeed, state-run banks reserve 86% of their credit for state enterprises, at least one-third of which are incurring losses and are saddled with bad debts. When private com-panies do receive bank loans, they are charged 4.5-6% a month; state companies pay 2.7% or less. Because of the shortage of credit, most private companies turn to friends, relatives or overseas Vietnamese, who charge as much as 10-12% a month.

Tapping foreign investors for cash is another avenue re-cently opened to the private sector, though few have taken the plunge. The government legalised joint ventures between foreign companies and local private enterprises in 1990, but 18 months later only three foreign firms had invested with

Vietnamese partners.

The largest such joint venture is between a small Japanese company and Au Quang Canh, a once-prosperous southern capitalist who had seven factories nationalised in 1975. The Japanese firm is investing US$140,000 to produce handicrafts in Ho Chi Minh City. There are two other joint ventures. One involves a Hongkong firm that is preparing to produce leather products in Haiphong. The other involves a Hungarian company, which is investing in the production of heat and sound-insulating sheets at a factory near Hanoi.

Most private entrepreneurs, however, are starting up trading outfits, which generate quick investment returns and offer some flexibility against the country's notorious inflation. Inflation has fallen from the triple-digit levels of the late 1980s, but it was still nearly 18% in 1992.

But even trade is often risky because of the volatility of Vietnam's currency. The value of the local unit fell to Dong 14,700:US$1 in December 1991 from Dong 7,000 at the beginning of the year, before rallying to Dong 10,500 by the end of 1992. Exporters who paid high rates for their products suffered huge losses when the dong suddenly strengthened.

Vietnamese products also face sharp competition from the annual invasion of at least US$500 million of cheap smuggled goods. This flood of goods often drives small private producers out of business.

But the vagaries of Vietnam's mixed economy are less troublesome than the almost insurmountable bureaucratic hurdles imposed by local officials. "The central government supports renovation, but a lot of officials still struggle against change," says Hai. "Localities try to keep their privileges, and many low-level officials use their positions to violate the law."

Many private companies find that the only way around junior bureaucrats is to form a joint venture with a state company. For instance, Thong Nhat Co., a small family-owned chain of shops selling construction materials in Hanoi, recently teamed up with a company belonging to the state's Science and Technology Commission.

Says Nguyen Cong, a Thong Nhat owner: "They have the right to import construction materials, but they have poor marketing skills. So we use their legal position to import construction materials and pay them for this relationship."

Bribes paid to government officials are also becoming a necessary business tool. "Corruption has opened up the party's ideology to allow the private economic sector [to] bring economic development," an economist says. "But now even the state sector has to pay money under the table to make business work."

Faced with these problems, perhaps the key demand of the private sector is the strengthening of the country's weak legal system. Businessmen say they desperately need laws to protect investment and to clarify property rights before they are willing to invest. Vietnam's lack of a system of business law or a civil code creates headaches for the business community.

"We have no commercial law to settle disputes between enterprises," Saigon Bank's Son says. "When businessmen sign contracts, they can't rely on legal texts, which allows them easily to cheat one another." The banker says many disputes cannot be settled by arbitration in courts because judges do not have any legal texts on which to base their judgments. "This means people are still cautious and conservative about investing," Son says.

Still, Vietnam's pioneering entrepreneurs are not giving up. The bitter, 61-year-old Thai, who stumbled in his first attempt to set up a private construction business in Hanoi, has received a licence to begin processing forestry products. He is awaiting an opportunity to return to the construction business.

New Landed Gentry

Amid poverty, house prices take off

HO CHI MINH CITY — As unlikely as it might seem, impoverished Vietnam is in the midst of a real-estate boom. Never mind that its ruling communist government — at least on paper — still forbids the sale of private property.

Foreign companies, enthusiastic about Vietnam's economic prospects, are arriving in droves to scout out real-estate projects. But most are still window-shopping, reluctant to invest because of the country's murky property laws or unable to raise financing because foreign banks remain wary about funding sizeable projects in Vietnam.

Property prices jumped as much as fivefold during 1992 in areas of Ho Chi Minh City, says an official of the city's Construction Department. A rundown, 400-square-metre villa in the centre of the city was on the market in October 1992 for just under US$600,000, up from only US$250,000 three months earlier.

"Some properties are now as expensive as those in Singapore or Sydney," observes an overseas Vietnamese businessman, who in early 1992 bought a small, dilapidated villa in Thu Duc, a northeastern suburb of Ho Chi Minh City, for US$35,000. By the end of the year, he was being offered US$120,000 for the house.

The official *Saigon Giai Phong* newspaper reported that 25,000 house sales had been registered in Ho Chi Minh City in the first nine months of 1992. In addition, nearly 10,000 new housing units had been built during the same period, the report added.

Some of the most feverish activity is taking place in An Phu and An Khanh, two communities lying just across the Saigon River from Ho Chi Minh City. They have been designated as future residential areas for foreigners.

Under Vietnamese law, all land belongs to the state and cannot be sold. But sellers circumvent the ban by building a small shack and then selling the rights to use the land under it. "We don't bother with the law," says one Vietnamese involved in real estate. "We hire specialists to fix our papers." These uncertain regulations have created vast new opportunities for corruption and threaten widespread land disputes in the future.

Property prices are also soaring in Hanoi. Villas built by the French colonialists on the city's main streets prior to 1954 were selling for US$820-1,025 per square metre in late 1992, up from US$205-245 three years earlier, says Dao Chan Hung of the House and Land Information Centre, the first official real-estate agency licensed to operate in the capital.

Prices in some parts of the city go up as much as 10% every 6-10 weeks, estimates Paul Fairhead, an Australian businessman who has spent more than two years exploring investment opportunities in Hanoi.

It is not just foreign demand that is fuelling the price surge. "When the state switched to a free-market economy [in the late 1980s], many private Vietnamese began making a lot of money, so the demand for bigger houses and shops increased," says Hung, the real-estate agent.

Much of the hot action has been sparked by speculation that the US will ease its trade embargo against Vietnam. "The real-estate business is highly feverish now, but it still hasn't come to a climax," observes a Vietnamese journalist who writes about economic developments. "This will only come a year after the US lifts the embargo."

Rents for foreigners leasing office or residential space are also surging, even though Vietnamese officials often claim that low costs are one of Vietnam's most important advantages over its neighbours. Japan's Nissho Iwai Corp. is renting a 250-square-metre villa from the Communist Party's Finance Department for US$13,000 a month, or about US$52 a square metre.

French villas rent from US$18 per square metre per month, with the tenant usually expected to pay the renovation costs himself. Even simple Vietnamese-style row houses begin at US$10 per square metre per month.

Rental fees in Ho Chi Minh City, Vietnam's economic hub, are even more exorbitant. Petronas, Malaysia's state-owned oil company, rented a small building in early 1992 for US$15,000 per month, with two years' rent paid in advance.

Hanoi's extravagant rates are due to a combination of factors: a desperate shortage of housing and office space resulting from an exploding population, destruction of parts of the city by US bombing during the Vietnam War and the communist Government's earlier mismanagement of its limited resources.

Hanoi, whose population rose from around 500,000 in the mid-1950s to roughly three million today, is one of Asia's most crowded cities. The capital's average resident has less than four square metres of living space. Ho Chi Minh City residents have about six square metres.

Wealth generated by the Communist Party's six-year reform programme has sparked a building boom throughout the country. Some 200,000 square metres of new housing were constructed in the capital in 1991 — roughly two-thirds by private builders — but this meets only a fraction of the city's needs, says Trinh Hong Trien, Hanoi's chief architect.

Much of Hanoi's construction boom is taking place in the suburbs of the capital, especially along Highway 1 south of the city and northeast along the road to the airport. But the survival of the city's ancient narrow "tube houses," with their curved, red-tiled roofs, is also threatened. Increasingly, these houses are being replaced by the same tall, flat-roofed shop houses with grate-metal doors that have become so popular in other Asian cities.

The Vietnamese Government since 1988 has issued licences to several dozen foreign companies interested in joint-

MURRAY HIEBERT

Yours for US$600,000: a house in Ho Chi Minh City.

venture real-estate projects. Some have renovated old hotels in Hanoi and Ho Chi Minh City, but only a handful of new construction projects have been launched, despite the country's desperate shortage of hotel rooms, offices and living space for foreigners.

Some of the biggest obstacles to investment in real-estate projects centre on the country's unclear legal framework, which makes it almost impossible for businessmen to find financing. Vietnam has not yet passed a mortgage law or a real-estate law and it has not yet introduced a land-title system.

"Everyone has faith in Vietnam's potential, but now there's still some big question marks," says a European businessman

139

who has spent 18 months in Ho Chi Minh City hammering out the details of a large commercial complex. "The biggest problem is that investors can't get financing. The lack of a mortgage law means you can't offer a bank the rights to your land if you default."

Foreign businessmen also say they need longer-term land leases. Most projects are licensed for only 20 years, which foreign investors say is too short to recoup their investment. They would prefer 99 years, but say they would be content with 50 years.

Because of these legal problems, many project holders are looking to resell their licences or are waiting for Hanoi to improve the legal climate. Still, a few, mostly small-scale projects are getting off the ground.

A French consortium completed renovations of the 109-room Pullman Metropole Hotel, Hanoi's first luxury hotel, in early 1992, and a Hongkong company has begun upgrading the 76-room Thang Long Hotel. Two office complexes, with space totalling roughly 60,000 square metres, and several small apartment buildings, with a total of 80-100 units, are nearly off the drawing board.

In Ho Chi Minh City, Taiwan's Yao Teh International Development Co. has renovated a 16-storey office building. But Richard Ellis, the international property firm that is managing the building, is having difficulty finding tenants willing to pay rents beginning at US$45 per square metre per month.

Hongkong's New World Group has begun constructing a US$63 million, 580-room hotel, the city's first new hotel since the communist victory 18 years ago. Another Hongkong firm has renovated the Century Saigon Hotel and an Australian company is operating the rebuilt Norfolk Hotel.

First Pacific Land, which is part of Indonesia's Salim Group, hopes to receive a licence in 1993 to build a US$75 million complex, including a hotel, offices and service apartments.

Second Time Lucky?

Foreign oil firms are bullish on Vietnam

HO CHI MINH CITY — Foreign oil companies have had little to cheer about from their offshore-exploration work in Vietnam. But hopes of a significant discovery have been refuelled by Hanoi's decision to put on the auction block potentially the largest oil field, along with 10 neighbouring concessions.

In December 1992, an Australian-Malaysian consortium won the right to develop the Dai Hung field, one of Southeast Asia's most promising oil fields off the coast of southern Vietnam. Broken Hill Proprietary (BHP) of Australia, in partnership with Petronas, Malaysia's state-owned oil company, beat out eight other companies or groups that had bid for the right to develop the field. The winning partnership expects to begin pumping oil by mid-1994.

Dai Hung was discovered in 1987 by Vietsovpetro, a Vietnamese-Russian joint venture that sank three wells close to where Mobil Corp. was drilling in 1975. That year's communist victory against the US-backed southern government forced the US oil giant to withdraw. Vietsovpetro, however, lacked the capital and technology to develop Dai Hung, and Hanoi was left with little choice but to open the field to other tenders.

"The opening up of Dai Hung to foreign companies marks a significant new development in Vietnam's oil industry," a representative of a foreign oil company says. "Before, PetroVietnam [state-owned Vietnam Oil & Gas Corp.] only added new acreage for exploration. Now, it's adding a discovered well."

A second flurry of activity erupted in early 1993 after the US had eased its trade embargo against Vietnam. In February, six teams from major US oil companies — which had anxiously watched from the sidelines while their competitors grabbed Vietnam's most promising blocks — arrived in Hanoi to hold talks with the Vietnamese.

The visiting US companies included Mobil, Unocal, Amoco, Exxon, Conoco and Marathon, according to Vietnamese officials. They say the American firms were vying for the Thanh Long, or Blue Dragon, field, which lies just east of Dai Hung and near the disputed area of the South China Sea that China has awarded to the US-based Crestone Energy Corp.

A foreign oil official says Thanh Long is one of the last promising areas in water depths of less than 200 metres. "Being so close to Dai Hung, it obviously has a lot of potential," he notes.

The easing of the American embargo in December 1992 allows US firms to sign contracts and begin seismic surveys and test drilling, although actual production must await a full lifting of the embargo. If Washington lifts its embargo in 1993, as many observers expect, the other option remaining for American companies will be farm-in arrangements with non-American firms already holding concessions.

Analysts believe Vietnam is interested in signing contracts with US firms for Thanh Long to gain some diplomatic protection in its dispute with China. Vietnam claims the Crestone block is located on its continental shelf, but China insists that it has rights to most of the South China Sea.

Foreign oil companies see their Vietnamese concessions as jewels in their crowns. A 1991 study by the Resource Systems Institute of the East-West Centre in Hawaii estimated Vietnam's oil reserves at 1.5-3 billion barrels, similar to the potential of Australia and Malaysia. The report forecast that Vietnam could be pumping 300-500,000 barrels per day (bpd) by 2005.

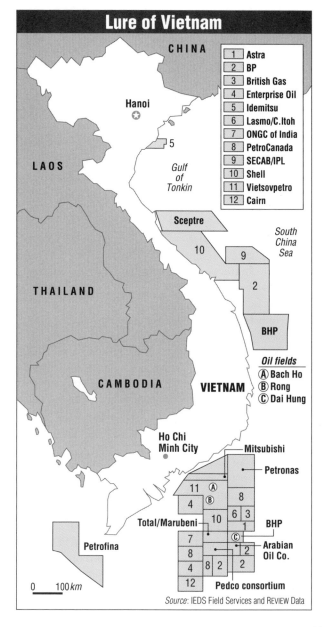

Lure of Vietnam

1	Astra
2	BP
3	British Gas
4	Enterprise Oil
5	Idemitsu
6	Lasmo/C.Itoh
7	ONGC of India
8	PetroCanada
9	SECAB/IPL
10	Shell
11	Vietsovpetro
12	Cairn

CHINA

Hanoi

LAOS

Gulf of Tonkin

THAILAND

Sceptre

South China Sea

CAMBODIA

VIETNAM

Oil fields
Ⓐ Bach Ho
Ⓑ Rong
Ⓒ Dai Hung

Ho Chi Minh City

Mitsubishi

Petronas

Total/Marubeni

BHP

Arabian Oil Co.

Petrofina

Pedco consortium

0   100 km

Source: IEDS Field Services and REVIEW Data

143

Nonetheless, both government officials and foreign oil-company executives admit that it is too early to give accurate figures on the country's oil potential. Dai Hung's reserves, for example, are estimated at 300-750 million barrels of recoverable crude. But there is a lot of uncertainty about this figure because of the oil field's complex geological structure and the outdated techniques used by exploration teams from the former Soviet Union.

The foreign oil firms that won the rights to develop Dai Hung face a major appraisal programme before they can begin production. "We know there's oil, but we still don't know how much or how to develop it," a foreign oil-company executive says.

After the final contract for developing the field is negotiated, oil sources say BHP will be entitled to 43.75% of the output, Petronas 20% and PetroVietnam 15%. The remaining 21.25% share was granted to Total of France and Sumitomo of Japan.

The only field currently producing oil in Vietnam is Bach Ho, or White Tiger, where the Vietnamese-Russian joint venture that was set up in 1981 is pumping about 106,000 bpd. In 1991, Vietsovpetro produced 11.2 million barrels from the field, all of which were exported to Japan and Singapore. The company produced nearly 40 million barrels in 1992.

Vietnamese officials privately complain about the outdated techniques used by the Russians, particularly what they view as a lack of concern about managing reserves and a failure to prevent severe rust on their platforms. But Do Quang Toan of the Ministry of Heavy Industry rejects rumours that Vietnam has plans to invite foreign oil companies to help Vietsovpetro exploit Bach Ho or Rong, a nearby oil field discovered by a Shell consortium in 1974.

The other focal point of interest involves five concessions considered to have significant potential because of their location near Dai Hung and Bach Ho. "The proximity to actual oil production makes these blocks more attractive and reduces the risk," a foreign oil-company executive says.

Vietsovpetro relinquished these blocks in late 1990, after

which the government decided to open the area to bids from foreign oil companies. In mid-1992, British Gas Exploration & Production was allotted the block closest to Dai Hung, while two other nearby blocks were awarded to Indonesia's Pt Astra Petronusa and to C. Itoh of Japan teaming up with Britain's Lasmo PLC. Mitsubishi Co. of Japan landed a block near the Bach Ho field. Another concession, just north of Mitsubishi's block, had not been offered by early 1993.

Five other nearby blocks, which had also been released by Vietsovpetro, were allotted in January 1992 to British Petroleum (BP) cooperating with Statoil of Norway; the Royal Dutch/Shell Group; France's Total teaming up with Marubeni of Japan and Norsk Hydro of Norway; Arabian Oil Co. of Japan, and a South Korean consortium. The consortium comprises Korea Petroleum Development Corp. (Pedco) and seven groups: Daewoo, Hyundai, Lucky-Goldstar, Samsung, Samhwan, Ssangyong and Daesung.

Because of the promising location of the 10 latest blocks, oil-industry analysts say Vietnam managed to drive up the cost of contracts substantially in the bidding. Signing bonuses for earlier production-sharing contracts had ranged from US$500,000-3 million, but during the last round, the South Korean consortium is believed to have beaten Britain's Enterprise Oil by offering as much as US$10 million. A Pedco official says the group paid less than this amount, but another South Korean industry executive says the signing bonus was in the US$7-9 million range.

Heavier data-viewing fees and more-expensive signing bonuses have prompted concern among foreign oil-company executives that Vietnam may be getting too greedy. "Some officials see the money handed over for licences as the main oil business," a foreign oil-company representative says. "There's a tendency to forget that the real money comes from oil production."

From mid-1988 until early 1993, Vietnam had signed 23 production-sharing contracts. Those who had signed prior to the recent frenzy include the Oil and Natural Gas Commission of India; Enterprise Oil; PetroCanada; Petrofina of Belgium; Petronas; Sceptre Resources of Canada; and a consortium led by SECAB of Sweden and International Petroleum of Canada.

By October 1992, these companies had drilled about 21 wells at a cost of more than US$300 million. The nine companies or groups granted licences in 1992 were expected over the next 18 months to complete seismic work and drill some 30 wells in what oil executives consider to be Vietnam's "most interesting areas."

None of the companies has found commercially exploitable oil. In 1991, Total relinquished its block in the northern Tonkin Gulf after drilling three wells. Petrofina kept only three of its eight blocks in the southwest after completing seismic surveys.

Petronas made a strike in late 1992 off the southern coast of Vietnam, but according to preliminary tests the well was believed to have only a modest 50-100 million barrels of oil. Enterprise made a strike two years earlier, but it had a flow of only 300 barrels a day. Shell and BP also had strikes with gas flows.

Foreign oil-company executives say other major companies are considering giving up some of their concession areas off the coast of central Vietnam and throwing their dice on the new blocks in the south. Several smaller companies are looking for partners with whom to share the cost of drilling exploration wells.

"In the first round, we've had no cause for big celebration," a foreign oil-company executive says. "If in the next round we get no goodies, there's a good chance you'll see a huge drop in interest here." He was referring to the fact that the current low price of less than US$20 for a barrel of oil has caused many companies to cut their exploration budgets.

Although many foreign investors in Vietnam are frustrated with a cumbersome bureaucracy and frequently changing regulations, foreign oil companies are surprisingly upbeat. "It's easy working in Vietnam," an executive says. "Setting up an office is the hardest thing. The bureaucracy here is less than in Indonesia. We can get clearance for a rig in less than a week." But the executive complains about the lack of airports, ports and modern roads as well as the country's over-extended service companies.

In an effort to cope with the flood of foreign oil companies, the government is working on the country's first oil law. In March 1992, a draft of the law, which defined the rights and obligations of Vietnamese and foreign parties, was presented to foreign oil-company representatives at an international seminar in the southern coastal town of Vung Tau.

Apparently in an attempt to increase the authority of PetroVietnam, the draft law also proposed to set up an independent petroleum-management authority under the control of the premier, Vo Van Kiet, rather than under the Ministry of Heavy Industry. The authority would establish oil policy, inspect drilling activities and redistribute exploration blocks. Many aspects of the draft law are modelled on the oil regulations of Indonesia and Malaysia.

Foreign oil-company executives, who give the government high marks for its oil-development strategy, welcome the move to regulate the emerging oil industry. But they disagree with the high rate of royalty fees on oil production — 6-25% depending on output — and a sharp 50% profits tax set in the draft law.

"It's a grab bag of all the taxes they could come up with," one foreign oil-company executive complains. "It's a bit worrying. Vietnam has to be careful not to price itself out of the exploration and production market."

The Ministry of Heavy Industry's Toan says the tax rates will be revised before the draft law is presented to the National Assembly. "Our target is to lure more foreign companies to come to Vietnam," he says. "Because of this, we have to balance the profits for Vietnam with the profits for foreign companies."

Chain Lending

Informal credit fills void left by banks

HO CHI MINH CITY — Tran Thi Be's living room, tucked behind a motorcycle repair shop in Ho Chi Minh City, hardly resembles a bank. Nor is it meant to. Yet dealers of motorcycle parts from the city's Tan Thanh market do not hesitate to visit her when they need loans or want to deposit money in savings accounts.

Be makes her living managing *hui* groups, or informal credit circles, which were popular throughout Asia before banks emerged. Despite the high risk, the 58-year-old Be has built a thriving enterprise with a seemingly endless supply of Vietnamese willing to invest their cash.

As an alternative to state-run banks, which lend up to 80% of their meagre assets to often troubled government-owned enterprises, Vietnamese are increasingly turning to credit circles and other alternative lending sources. Analysts say the credit circles took off in a big way after the Communist Party began its drive towards a free-market economy seven years ago, though it is difficult to know how many exist because of their informal nature.

According to government estimates, only 6% of Vietnam's 71 million people borrow from, or deposit in, formal financial institutions. "I never use banks," says Hoang Le Quy, a property developer in Hanoi who participates in three credit circles. "I don't trust them. In other countries, it's easy to withdraw money from the bank, but in Vietnam it's very difficult."

Although credit circles are small, they have played an

148

Vietnamese are turning away from banks for credit.

important role in firing up Vietnam's modest economic recovery. A government economist estimates that up to 40% of the credit in rural areas and as much as 60% in cities is provided by credit circles. "As long as the banking system is not developed," the economist says, "these groups will flourish like mushrooms after the rain."

Be runs at least seven credit circles at any one time. A typical group has 10 members, each of whom deposits Dong 20,000 (US$1.90) daily. After 10 days, the group has a kitty of Dong 2 million, which is given to the member who has pledged to pay the highest amount of interest — perhaps the equivalent of 10-20% a month — to the other members. But the principal is not repaid.

Members deposit their money each day. At the end of the second 10-day period, Be, as the group organiser, gets to use the second Dong 2 million pool interest-free. Every 10 days, another person receives the funds until the cycle is completed.

Members of Be's groups who borrow the money first

benefit from gaining access to Dong 2 million after only paying in Dong 200,000. Later kitty users profit from being paid interest by the other members.

Be sold used cars and motorcycles before the communist victory in 1975. Anticipating that her business would be shut down by the country's new rulers, she switched to selling motorcycle parts. In 1983, Be started up her first credit circle for fellow shopkeepers.

"All members of my credit circles need money to re-stock their shops," Be explains. "But it's difficult for them to ask for credit from the bank because of the complicated procedures. It takes at least a week to get a loan, during which time they can miss many business opportunities."

Like other credit circles in Vietnam, Be's groups are managed without any paper work, collateral or state regulations. As a result, Be admits only merchants — mostly women — whom she knows. But even then, some of her groups have collapsed because a member has disappeared or has faced a business failure.

Many different types of credit circles have sprung up in Vietnam. Some have working money pools of Dong 200 million or more. Others in poor rural areas might have pooled only 400 kilograms of rice that is sold by members.

Credit circles have emerged in response to the desperate shortage of capital available from the country's banks for private business or farming activities. According to a recent study of private companies conducted by the government's Central Institute for Economic Management, only 8% of the private businesses in Hanoi and 18% of those in Ho Chi Minh City are able to get bank loans.

The credit crunch is equally critical in rural areas. In 1992, the Bank for Agriculture expanded its lending policies to provide short-term loans of Dong 2.4 trillion to 2 million farming households, or 20% of the total. But the Ministry of Agriculture estimates that 64% of the country's farming families need credits to buy such badly needed things as fertiliser and pesticides.

But credit circles only benefit Vietnamese with enough

money to deposit regularly in the money pools. In the countryside, many peasants often have to turn to wealthy neighbours for cash advances to buy fertiliser.

Foreign non-governmental relief agencies have found cases in which peasants have paid interest rates of up to 50-70% for four-month cash advances. As a result, many peasants use only half the normal fertiliser or pesticide required for a crop. In a rising number of cases, heavily indebted peasants are losing their land and are being forced to work for richer neighbours.

In cities, Vietnamese too poor to participate in credit circles often turn to pawnshops, where they are charged up to 1% interest daily or 20% a month. "It's the worst form of capitalist lending," says an overseas Vietnamese businessman working in Ho Chi Minh City.

Several recently opened commercial and stockholding banks in Ho Chi Minh City have simplified their loan procedures in an effort to play a greater role in providing credit to the private sector. But they have only limited available capital.

Huynh Buu Son, deputy managing director of Saigon Bank for Industry and Trade, estimates that new bank credit in 1992 totalled only Dong 4-6 trillion. He says this figure is small because the government limits credit expansion to control inflation.

Until the banking situation improves, credit circles are likely to find even more success, especially if Vietnam's economy continues to improve. "The credit circles play a very important role in our economy," says Quy, the real-estate developer who uses his investment earnings to buy and repair old houses. "People with a lot of money use the groups to save money, and people with no money get access to some credit."

Economic Upturn

Free-market reforms help, but perils remain

HANOI — Vietnam's economic reformers finally have something to cheer about.

The country's economy made a surprisingly strong recovery in 1992, escaping the clutches of disaster that many had predicted following the abrupt loss of aid and trade with the former Soviet-led communist bloc a year earlier. Despite the US trade embargo, the country managed to chalk up its first foreign-trade surplus in recent memory. It also curbed inflation, while its currency rallied, rice production burgeoned and foreign investment surged.

Vietnam began its moves from a centrally planned to a market economy in 1986. Since then, Hanoi has allowed farm cooperatives to collapse and has taken its first halting steps towards privatising some inefficient state-owned enterprises. The private sector has developed quickly, accounting for nearly three-quarters of the country's gross domestic product by 1992.

Despite the good news, serious perils remain. Money-losing state companies still drain government coffers, while poor tax collection exacerbates the budget deficit, threatening to fuel another round of inflation.

Unemployment has grown as overstaffed state enterprises have been forced to shed workers. Corruption has hobbled the reform effort, while rampant smuggling threatens local industry and causes critical losses of state revenue. Bureaucratic bottlenecks and frequently changing regulations slow foreign investment. The country's export base remains narrow and weak rice prices threaten agricultural output.

These difficulties were exacerbated in 1991 by the abrupt collapse of the Soviet Union. The Soviets had controlled more than half of Vietnam's foreign trade and had provided Vietnam with more than US$1 billion a year in aid and concessionary trade arrangements. Hanoi rallied by turning to its neighbours in Asia to replace its former Soviet patron.

Vietnam's exports in 1992 reached US$2.45 billion, up roughly 24% from a year earlier, when the trade crisis was at its height. Imports totalled US$2.38 billion, resulting in a US$70 million trade surplus, a major feat for a country in which imports outstripped exports by four to one a decade ago.

Singapore, Japan and Hongkong, which together accounted for more than half of Vietnam's trade since 1991, were the biggest beneficiaries of the chaos in the former Soviet Union. Singapore, which lifted its ban on investment in Vietnam following the Cambodian peace agreement, has become Vietnam's largest trading partner with two-way trade in 1992 reaching US$1.46 billion, up from only US$111 million three years earlier, according to Vietnamese statistics.

Japan's trade with Vietnam rose to US$667 million in 1992, more than double the figure three years earlier, largely because Japan buys four-fifths of Vietnam's crude oil.

Vietnam's export base, however, remained narrow. Three-quarters of its export earnings were generated by two items. Unprocessed farm products accounted for 40%, with rice exports nearly doubling to 1.9 million tonnes. This surge helped Vietnam hold onto its four-year title as the world's third-largest rice exporter. Another third of its export earnings came from crude-oil sales, which rose to 5.4 million tonnes from 3.9 million tonnes in 1991.

Much of Vietnam's success in finding new markets is due to foreign trade reforms introduced since 1989. Hanoi has abolished most trade quotas, decontrolled export and import prices and adopted a more realistic exchange rate based on market forces. The government also has increased the number of companies allowed to engage in direct foreign trade.

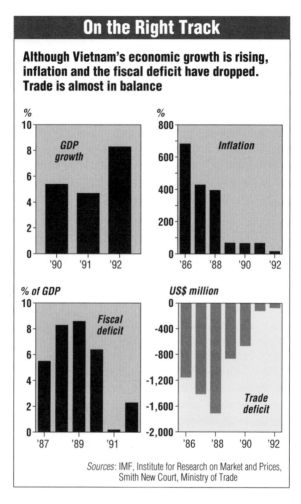

On the Right Track

Although Vietnam's economic growth is rising, inflation and the fiscal deficit have dropped. Trade is almost in balance

Sources: IMF, Institute for Research on Market and Prices, Smith New Court, Ministry of Trade

But exporters are still hobbled by the country's desperate shortage of working capital. Hanoi also has had troubled finding new capitalist buyers for such products as rubber, coffee, garments and handicraft items, which traditionally had been sold to its former Soviet ally.

Thanks to good weather, grain production reached nearly 24 million tonnes in 1992, up from the previous year's record harvest of 21.7 million tonnes. The bumper crop was a mixed blessing, however. The government's efforts to control monetary growth caused a shortage of capital to buy rice, both for export and for internal use.

As a result, huge surpluses built up, particularly in the fertile Mekong delta in the South, causing rice prices to fall to Dong 900-1,000 (8.5-9.5 US cents) a kilogramme by late 1992. While this played a major role in stabilising inflation, it demoralised farmers, who were not able to cover their production costs. Some Vietnamese economists feared that farmers would cut production unless prices rise to about Dong 1,200 a kilogramme.

Rice production in Vietnam has jumped since 1988, due to the government's decision to abandon inefficient farm cooperatives and return land to private tillers. The reforms also allowed market forces to drive up the artificially low price of agricultural products, while the government invested large sums of money in opening new fields and expanding irrigation systems, particularly in the Mekong delta.

Inflation, which averaged nearly 70% in 1990 and 1991, fell to roughly 18% in 1992. Economists attributed the sharp drop to the government's efforts to reduce the budget deficit and end subsidised credit for money-losing state enterprises.

But prices of some commodities rose much faster than others. Economists estimate that prices of industrial goods rose 36% in 1992, while those of farm products fell 19%. "Farmers are the only losers," one economist says. "They have to sell 50% more rice and tomatoes to buy the same manufactured goods."

The continuing large budget deficit, which in the past had been covered by credits from Moscow, threatened to fuel further inflation. Vietnamese economists estimate that the deficit would double in 1993 to Dong 9 trillion, which equals roughly 7% of GDP and 35% of the government's expected revenue.

Officials say the government would cover the deficit by borrowing from state banks, rather than by printing more money, as it had in the past. The government also sold Dong

800 billion of treasury bonds in the first half of 1992, which soaked up excess liquidity and raised funds for capital projects such as the 1,500 kilometre north-south electricity line.

Royalties on growing crude-oil exports partially have offset the loss of aid from the former Soviet Union. But the government still faces the difficulty of establishing a new tax system to replace cash transfers from state enterprises as the main source of government revenue. Smuggling, estimated at over US$300 million in illegal imports each year, deprives the government of additional tax income.

The International Monetary Fund (IMF) reports that the government cut its spending to 11% of GDP in 1991 from 19% three years earlier. Much of this saving resulted from sharp cuts in capital expenditures, such as development of the country's still-backward infrastructure, and the freezing of wages for state employees, whose real salaries fell 65% between 1990 and 1992 due to inflation.

The currency rose 15% in 1992, to Dong 10,500 to the US dollar. This was a sharp reversal from 1991, when it lost nearly half of its value as Vietnam struggled to find hard currency to buy imports that had long been supplied by Moscow.

The dong's surge reflected Vietnam's success in balancing trade, restricting money-supply growth and increasing production, coupled with massive support operations from the central bank. In late 1991 and early 1992, the State Bank of Vietnam sold locally more than US$200 million in foreign exchange and gold to halt the currency's collapse.

But Vietnamese businessmen fret that the stronger currency is hurting foreign trade. Economists predict that the export of products other than crude oil and rice will stagnate unless the currency weakens to around Dong 12,000 to the dollar.

Hanoi during 1992 tentatively began preparing to partially privatise state firms, with the hope of reducing the burden on the government of having to prop up ailing companies. Officials hoped the plan would inject private capital into struggling industries, improve their management and increase efficiency.

The proposed programme had earlier faced considerable opposition from Communist Party conservatives. "Some officials believe privatisation will undermine the socialist cornerstone of our economy and begin our deviation toward capitalism," observes a technocrat who helped draft the experimental programme.

The first experimental privatisation plan did not go smoothly. Six of the original seven companies proposed for the project were dropped from the Finance Ministry's list because of opposition from workers or managers. Economists say managers wanted to avoid the control of a board of directors, while many workers feared they would lose their jobs.

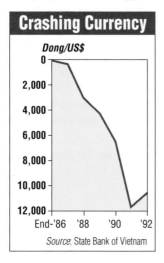

Crashing Currency

Dong/US$

Source: State Bank of Vietnam

The one remaining company, Legamex, had the most modern facilities and was the only company with significant exports, which totalled US$20 million in 1991. Four foreign companies expressed interest in buying shares in the company, but the government rejected the plan.

Potential local investors were unenthusiastic about the pilot privatisation scheme, at least in part because the government insisted on retaining 30% control of privatised firms, Vietnamese economists report.

Meanwhile, industrial production, which had fallen roughly 5% in each of the three previous years, surged nearly 15% in 1992. But this rise was fuelled by a few key sectors, with oil up 40%; chemical fertilisers, 25%; and cement, nearly 20%.

Despite the gains in industrial production, some manufacturers were struggling to survive. These included producers of textiles, bicycles, electric fans and other light industrial products that were hit by the flood of cheap goods smuggled across the border from China.

In Ho Chi Minh City, the nine factories belonging to the Union of Hong Gam Textile Mills were stockpiling several million metres of unsold cloth in late 1992, even though they had dropped their prices by one-third in an attempt to compete with cheaper Chinese products.

Vietnam News, an official daily, reported in September 1992 that Vietnamese manufacturers had built up an inventory of more than Dong 350 billion of goods since March, largely because of the flood of Chinese products that began after the normalisation of Sino-Vietnamese relations in late 1991.

Unemployment was another problem. An estimated 5 million workers, or 28% of the rural workforce, are underemployed, while 3.5 million people in cities, or 22% of the urban workforce, have no jobs. In addition, the population continues growing more quickly than new jobs can be created.

Foreign investors continued coming, with the government issuing licences for 555 projects valued at US$4.6 billion by the end of 1992. But actual disbursements remained slow due to the country's bureaucratic bottlenecks and weak infrastructure.

Only US$1.2 billion actually had been spent in the five years prior to the end of 1992, and more than one-third of this had been disbursed by foreign companies exploring for oil off Vietnam's southern coast. During this period, foreign firms had recruited only 20,000 Vietnamese workers.

Early in 1992 — in an apparent effort to spark increased foreign investment — Hanoi granted licences authorising the first six foreign banks to open branches in Vietnam since the communist victory in 1975. Officials also hoped that the foreign branches would speed modernisation of the country's still antiquated banking system.

Banque Indosuez of France and Bangkok Bank were the first two foreign banks to open in Ho Chi Minh City in July. They were followed by three French banks — Banque

Francaise du Commerce Exterieur, Banque Nationale de Paris and Credit Lyonnais from France — and Australia & New Zealand Bank.

But excitement surrounding the opening of these branches was muted when the State Bank announced that it had increased the level of capital the foreign banks must leave in the country, sharply driving up the costs of their operations. Instead of being able to repatriate the minimum US$15 million capital requirement after opening their branches, the banks were told they had to deposit 70% of this money in Vietnamese banks at low interest rates.

Despite Vietnam's success in overcoming the 1991 crisis, economic growth — although estimated at 8.3% in 1992 — remains chaotic and slow. With the continuing US trade embargo, Vietnam has a hard time attracting the investment capital needed to rebuild the country's shattered infrastructure and boost economic growth.

Premier Vo Van Kiet told the National Assembly in late 1992 that the country would need investment worth US$4 billion over the next eight years if it hoped to double GDP by 2000. Some US allies, including Japan, France, Italy and Australia, have resumed aid to Vietnam since it withdrew its troops from Cambodia. And Washington announced in July 1993 that it would no longer block loans from the IMF and World Bank.

No Dong, No Deal

Corruption spreading rapidly in the north

HANOI — Angry residents of Quang Loc village, south of Hanoi, decided in early 1992 that they had had enough of their local leaders.

These corrupt officials were pocketing the lion's share of the peasants' agricultural tax payments, overcharging them for electricity and allowing relatives to use the village's best communal land. Frustrated that they could not get the central government to help rein in their "little kings," the farmers took the law into their own hands.

A respected army lieutenant colonel was living in retirement in their village. With his encouragement, the villagers hatched a plot to arrest the local Communist Party boss, the village chief and his deputy, the police chief and the head of

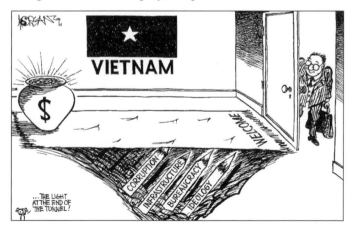

the agricultural department. But their plan was only partially successful. Two of the officials got wind of it and fled before they could be picked up.

Several months after their arrest, the three other officials remained in the hands of the villagers. Hanoi had sent in police reinforcements on several occasions, but attempts to rescue the detainees had failed. The peasants had built a fence around the village and threatened to kill their hostages if anyone tried to free them.

This incident in Quang Xuong district of Thanh Hoa province highlights the growing popular frustration at increasing corruption in Vietnam. Although Hanoi mounted a campaign in June 1990 to combat corruption, many Vietnamese claim the problem has worsened in the past few years.

Hanoi residents say it is now virtually impossible to find a job, get a licence to build a house, receive treatment in a hospital, get a child into a nursery school, obtain a visa to travel abroad, or secure a business or import-export licence without paying bribes.

The director of a private trading company selling imported Chinese agricultural equipment in Hanoi says he gets four to 10 "uninvited guests" each month from various police and government offices. Each visit costs him around Dong 50,000 (US$4.50). Truck drivers complain that they are stopped up to 30 times on a trip from Ho Chi Minh City in the south to Hanoi in the north. Each time they have to pay up before they are allowed to continue their trip.

This increasing corruption is not only hampering economic development but also destroying public confidence in party and government, warned *Dai Doan Ket*, a weekly newspaper of the Vietnam Fatherland Front — an umbrella organisation comprising women's groups, youth associations and other bodies.

Although corruption is widespread in many countries of Southeast Asia, it is a relatively new phenomenon in northern Vietnam, which has been under communist rule since 1954. Party officials appear gradually to have lost much of their revolutionary discipline and have become more interested in personal profit.

The labour union bi-weekly, *Lao Dong*, reported in 1991 that the courts in the north tried only five to seven cases of corruption each year during the Vietnam wars. But by 1985 — when the party launched reforms to move the country to a free-market economy — the number of cases had increased 1,800% from 1976; by 1988 they had soared by 2,230%.

While corruption is rapidly spreading in the north, most Vietnamese and foreign observers believe it is still worse in the former capitalist south, which has more money and is located far from the central government.

Many Vietnamese say corruption and abuse is worst at the provincial, district and village level. "In local areas, the party chief is the most powerful person — he's a dictator," one party official says. "He brings all his relatives into the government, so corruption is biggest there."

State Inspector Nguyen Ky Cam, one of the key officials responsible for battling white-collar crime, told the English-language *Vietnam News* in late 1991 that his office had investigated 5,070 cases of corruption in the previous 18 months. They had cost the state Dong 1,730 billion, 2,235 taels of gold (worth Dong 10.3 billion) and over 36,000 tonnes of rice. He said disciplinary action had been taken against 19,220 state employees, including six vice-ministers.

Cam attributed the problem to the government's lack of laws as the party moved from the old Soviet-style subsidised economic system to a free-market economy. In addition, the bureaucracy remains cumbersome; numerous offices have overlapping responsibilities for the same task, allowing frequent opportunities for abuse, Cam said.

Low salaries add to the problem. "A traffic policeman only earns Dong 70,000 a month, so he has to steal money from people to care for his family," a journalist points out. Many Vietnamese call the police "daytime robbers," because of their habit of stopping motorcycles and cars at unofficial roadblocks and demanding money.

In addition, the party appears reluctant to punish its officials. Because of relationships built up during years of revolutionary struggle, the party remains an elite "old boys' network." Nobody advances in the system without what the Vietnamese call an "umbrella" — a higher-ranking patron who provides protection for his proteges.

The party daily, *Nhan Dan*, said in early 1992 that the lenient sentences imposed on convicted officials were another reason corruption could not be curtailed. The paper cited the case of a bank official in Lang Son, near the Chinese border, who received only a three-year suspended sentence for his role in a smuggling deal involving Dong 240 million. The surprisingly candid *Nhan Dan* article attributed this leniency to the lack of an independent legal system. It said "judges and members of the jury are under very strong pressure from local party organisations or governments" and charged that judges "manipulate the law at will."

Whistle-blowers who call attention to corruption are often punished, further hobbling the battle against graft. Three people were expelled from the party in 1991 after filing charges against village officials in Dong Nai province in the south who were illegally selling land and pocketing state funds intended for a new economic zone, *Lao Dong* reported. The whistle-blowers were accused of "intending to overthrow the government and destroying internal solidarity."

Just What the Doctor Ordered

Private clinics provide superior health care

HANOI — Ly Nam De Street, often referred to as "army street" because of its concentration of military offices and housing for officers' families, is rapidly gaining a new reputation for its quality private health care.

Five private clinics have opened for business along this crowded street in the capital of Vietnam, whose Communist Party long held free, state-supplied medical care as a central plank of its domestic policy.

The hundreds of private medical facilities that have opened across the country in recent years are among a series of moves instituted by the government to breathe new life into a deteriorating health system. It is suffering from shortages of medicine and declining morale among its doctors and nurses.

Some of the small private clinics are run by people like Le Van Hien, a 67-year-old doctor who retired after serving in the army for 40 years, including a stint with Vietnamese troops in Cambodia. Others are known as "after-hours" clinics because they are staffed by doctors who first put in eight hours in government hospitals. Both types of clinics require licences to operate and the Ministry of Health has set maximum fees that they can charge.

"Two kinds of people come to see me," says Hien, who examines patients on a couch in the living room of his tiny house in an army officers' compound just off Ly Nam De Street. "Some people have gone to a state hospital but didn't get good service, so they come here to get diagnosed. Others don't want to travel so far from their homes."

Most medical experts give Vietnam's communist government high marks for its success in improving health care after the defeat of French colonial rule in 1954, when the country had only 51 doctors to serve a population of about 20 million. It mounted a mass vaccination campaign against epidemic diseases such as typhoid and cholera, and urged people to dig latrines and wells, drink boiled water and improve village hygiene and sanitation. Hanoi began training large numbers of health workers, and by 1965 roughly two-thirds of the villages in the northern provinces had trained assistant doctors.

Today's health-care crisis began not long after the communist north's victory over the US-backed south in 1975. Within four years, the country faced severe food shortages and its economy was on the brink of collapse because of the party's rapid drive to implement socialism and the cut-off in foreign aid following Hanoi's 1979 invasion of Cambodia.

The country's economy has improved since free-market reforms were introduced in 1986, but health care has continued to suffer due to shortages of medicine and foreign exchange with which to import supplies. The southern capital Ho Chi Minh City, the best-supplied area of the country, has just two drug factories — joint ventures with Roussel Uclaf and Rhone-Poulenc of France. They produce about 40% of the city's needs, according to Duong Quang Trung, the city's director of health services.

The city imports medicines valued at US$5 million, but that is only a fraction of the US$80 million imported by the US-backed southern government in the 1970s, Trung says. He estimates that the nearly 2 million overseas Vietnamese, most of whom had fled the country since the communist victory in 1975, send another US$15-20 million of medicines each year to their families back home. Most of these drugs are sold to the city's 1,300 licensed private pharmacies, whose numbers have exploded since they were legalised in 1989.

Hanoi's Ministry of Health has achieved impressive results in the past three decades by establishing more than

9,000 communal health stations throughout the country and training over 23,000 doctors, or about 3.4 per 10,000 people. That compares with an average of 1.8 per 10,000 in other low-income countries. But foreign analysts contend these figures are misleading: few health workers are at their jobs full time and many of the local clinics are empty shells with meagre medical supplies, limited budgets, high rates of staff absenteeism and few patients.

The Phuoc Long health station, located about 10 kilometres east of Ho Chi Minh City, has a staff of eight trained medical workers, but it treats an average of only 10 patients a day, according to its director, Le Minh Ky. Ky says most of his staff have to supplement their salaries of roughly Dong 50,000 (about US$4.50) a month by setting up small shops, raising pigs or farming.

"If you go to a health clinic in a commune you have to make an appointment in advance or else nobody will be there," says Nguyen Thi Ngoc Phuong, director of the Tu Du Women's Hospital in Ho Chi Minh City. "The staff spend one or two hours in the clinic each day and then they go to the rice fields to raise money to feed their families."

Says one foreign relief official who provides aid to the health sector: "Vietnam's health system is great on paper — there are health stations in most communes and there are personnel in place. But there's a serious lack of basic medical supplies. If clinics have nothing to offer, people don't expect anything and stop coming."

Health-care services in poor, remote areas of the country are even more limited than those in urban areas. The Swedish International Development Authority conducted a survey in 1989 in Ha Tuyen province, along the Chinese border. It found that 76% of farming women and 40% of women working in forestry had not gone anywhere for health treatment the last time they were ill. More than two-thirds of the women said they had to travel more than one hour for ante-natal care.

The government's legislation of private health care was an attempt to resuscitate the country's flagging medical system. "The advantage of the new regulation is that it allows us to set up a network of first aid health care in many neighbourhoods," says Nguyen Ba Kinh, the head surgeon at Bach Mai Hospital, the capital's largest medical facility.

But Kinh says he was worried that the policy change would cause further deterioration of services in state hospitals, because doctors would leave their government jobs early and put more energy into private practices, where they could earn two or three times their state salaries in a few hours.

The government also has introduced a system of hospital fees in an effort to supplement its health budget. The budget was estimated at US$142 million, roughly 3.7% of total state spending, or just over US$2 per person, according to a January 1990 economic report prepared by the UN Development Programme and Vietnam's State Planning Committee.

The fees are low: a normal birth in Ho Chi Minh City costs Dong 5,000 and stomach surgery in Hanoi costs Dong 30,000. Several categories of people, including civil servants and war veterans, are exempted from paying. But the new charges have contributed to hospital-bed occupancy rates falling from 100% to roughly 60-80% in the past few years, according to Vietnamese doctors and foreign medical experts.

Observers are still uncertain whether the introduction of fees is forcing many sick people to go without treatment — or whether they are going to private doctors. "I fear the poor will lose access to health care," says Phuong of Tu Du Hospital.

Fred Abbatt of Britain's Health Manpower Systems carried out a study of Vietnamese health care for the Swedish authority in 1989. He concluded that the demands on hospitals also have decreased because of the wider availability of drugs on the free market, the impact of the government's child-immunisation programme and improving nutrition. With assistance from Unicef and the UN's World Health Organisation (WHO), Vietnam has launched a massive immunisation drive in the past five years that increased the immunisation coverage for children under one year to 70% by the end of 1989, according to WHO.

Although many foreign analysts believe these figures are overly optimistic, they do agree that the government's recent efforts to control infectious diseases played an important role in reducing infant mortality to about 50 per 1,000, according to a 1988 demographic and health survey conducted with UN assistance.

Increasing food production also has contributed to the decreasing demand for hospital beds. But while more rice is available, the lack of adequate nutrition continues to plague a large number of people, according to a 1990 study by Tu Giay, director of the National Institute of Nutrition in Hanoi. Giay found the average Vietnamese still gets only 1,932 calories a day — or roughly 15% less than the WHO-recommended level of 2,300 — with nearly 25% of those surveyed getting less than 1,800 calories. Roughly half of Vietnam's children are undernourished, with more than 14% suffering from severe malnutrition.

Anthem of Sorrows

Composer's music can again be heard

HANOI — The popular music of Van Cao can be heard again in Vietnam. But this new freedom has come a little late for the 70-year-old composer of Vietnam's militaristic national anthem.

"I regret that I was not asked to contribute to my country," says the ailing artist, whose works were banned for 30 years because he criticised Communist Party excesses in the late 1950s. "Now when I enjoy the freedom to create, my health is so poor."

The party quietly lifted the ban on the work of Van Cao, who is also a celebrated poet and painter, when it mounted a reform campaign in 1987 to shift the country towards a free-market economy and grant more freedom to artists. "No one came to say I was now free, but they suddenly began organising Van Cao music nights," the composer says.

Van Cao.

Sixty-seven performances of his music were held throughout the country in 1987, and the government-controlled media again began publishing his poems and line drawings. "In Vietnam, when people want to admit a mistake, they try to correct it in secret," Van Cao says. "We kiss and make up in the bedroom."

But a few former party leaders responsible for the artist's years of isolation have made some attempts to reconcile with Van Cao. Shortly before his death in October 1990, Le Duc Tho — for decades one of the dominant figures in the Vietnamese Communist Party and the official who first convinced the composer to join the party in the 1940s — invited Van Cao to his house. "Tho didn't apologise, but he said life was long so everyone can make mistakes," Van Cao recalls.

Van Cao's troubles began in 1957 — three years after the communists defeated the French forces — when he and other writers founded a humanist literature movement that wilted like the Hundred Flowers campaign in China.

The group began publishing a literary journal, *Nhan Van*, which criticised the party's land-redistribution programme under which thousands of landlords were killed. "It was reasonable for intellectuals to have strong reactions to those mistakes, which had killed the basis for our revolution," Van Cao says.

Apparently fearing that the group's ideas would spread, the party arrested around 40 of its members, including about a dozen poets and writers. Some were tried and sentenced to prison terms and their works were destroyed.

Van Cao stayed out of jail, but he was ordered to stop using his pen. "They banned my painting, my art and my participation in culture, because I was a spokesman for those who love liberty," he says. "Thirty years without poetry was like 30 years in prison."

The artist survived by writing musical scores for movies, selling small line drawings to newspapers and working in a theatre. Despite his ordeal, Van Cao says he was never ousted from the party, nor did he resign.

Van Cao grew up in the northern port city of Haiphong in the 1920s and his early life near the sea continues to play a dominant role in his music. "I understand life through rivers and waves," he says, explaining why many of his poems refer to the sea or rivers.

Another feature of Van Cao's style is the influence of Roman Catholic and classical European music on traditional

Vietnamese music forms. The artist, whose family was Buddhist, picked up foreign ideas at a French Catholic school, where he was a choirboy.

Van Cao went to study at the Indochinese art school in Hanoi. He says the severe famine during the Japanese occupation — in which over 1 million people are thought to have died — prompted him in 1944 to join the Viet Minh revolutionary movement to end over 80 years of French rule.

Shortly after Van Cao arrived at the Viet Bac base near the Chinese border, the Viet Minh asked him to write a song to encourage the soldiers. He soon produced "Forward March!":

Our flag red with the blood of victory bears the spirit of our country
The road to glory passes over the bodies of our foes
Forward! All together, advance!
Our Vietnam is strong and eternal.

"I wanted a song that was so simple that it could be understood by everyone — from children to peasants," he says. Five days before Ho Chi Minh declared independence on 2 September 1945, he chose Van Cao's song as the national anthem.

In the early 1980s, there was a competition to choose a new national anthem. In the end, none of the entries were deemed to be of high enough quality to replace the one written by Van Cao.

When playing the piano today, Van Cao often pounds on the keyboard with his fists and elbows. He says he does that because the fingers on his right hand are stiff from an injury suffered in a bicycle accident in the 1960s. But he admits the angry-sounding style also fit his frustration after his art was banned.

Showboat
To Hanoi

Water puppet theatre has a pool for a stage

HANOI — The firecrackers start to sizzle and pop as soon as the lights dim. With a great splash, two brightly coloured dragon puppets pop out of the water and another performance begins.

Welcome to Hanoi's Water Puppet Theatre. With a pool of water as their stage, dozens of puppets cavort above the shimmering surface for the next hour, choreographed by hidden puppet masters who hover below, immersed in the pool.

Audiences still flock to see these raucous plays depicting scenes of peasants planting rice, catching fish or protecting their ducks from a prowling fox, which defiantly scampers up a tree after capturing his prey. The audience howls with delight as a fisherman misses his catch and plops a basket onto the head of an unsuspecting colleague passing in a boat. This water puppet theatre in Hanoi may well be the longest-running theatrical performance in Asia.

The puppets, some of which stand half-a-metre tall, are painted in bright colours and constructed from a special light wood that can resist constant exposure to water. They are manipulated with long bamboo poles by puppeteers who stand in a metre of water behind a bamboo curtain in a red-tiled building, symbolising an ancient village communal house. These days the puppeteers wear rubber diving suits, but in the past they fought off the cold of Hanoi's harsh winters by drinking *nuoc mam*, fermented fish sauce.

For a sense of drama during battle scenes or dragon dances, firecrackers explode out of the water, spewing smoke and churning up the surface of the water. Vietnamese folk opera singers — accompanied by traditional instruments such as the bamboo flute, bronze drum, stone gong and bamboo xylophone — cue the audience on the story line.

The history of the water puppet theatre, like so much in Vietnam, is inseparable from politics. Ho Chi Minh, the still widely revered founder of communist Vietnam, ordered the establishment of the water puppet theatre in 1956, two years after his forces defeated the French colonial army. "His goal was to bring a smile to the face of children," says Dang Anh Nga, deputy director of the theatre. Weekly performances have continued ever since, except for interruptions in the late 1960s and early 1970s, when Hanoi was emptied to escape US bombs.

Water puppetry is a folk art unique to northern Vietnam. Historians say Vietnamese peasants began performing water puppet shows more than 800 years ago during festivals celebrating the end of the spring rice harvest. A stele erected in 1121 at a pagoda south of Hanoi depicts a water puppet performance for a monarch of the Ly dynasty, which unified different principalities of northern Vietnam after nearly 1,000 years of Chinese rule.

Art in Vietnam has been made to serve politics time and again over the past four decades — first by the party seeking to build popular support for socialism and its war against the US, and then by artists critical of the party's post-war bungling and its corrupt officials. But the content of water puppetry has remained largely apolitical. Nga attributes this to the fact that the puppets are able to depict only a very simple story line, which leaves much to the imagination.

In the past 10 years, the water puppet troupe has performed in France, Italy, the Netherlands, Switzerland, Australia and Japan. Nga says one of the biggest difficulties in performing abroad is recreating the scenes involving fireworks, because airlines do not allow explosives on board and fireworks experts refuse to reveal their secret formulas. As a result, the troupe has to bring fireworks specialists along when it travels overseas.

Adding Up Costs Of Dissent

Mathematician challenges party ideology

HANOI — Phan Dinh Dieu gets away with saying things few other Vietnamese dare utter in public. The 56-year-old mathematician calls on the ruling Communist Party to abandon its Marxist-Leninist ideology and challenges it to allow other parties to compete in the country's political life.

Dieu believes Vietnam remains in a deep state of crisis, despite the party's six-year reform programme. He charges that abuses of power, corruption and smuggling are increasing, while health care, education and living standards generally continue to decline. He is convinced the only way out of this crisis is for the party to introduce wide-ranging political reforms.

Phan Dinh Dieu.

"Some people think democracy is a luxury for a poor country like Vietnam and say we need more food, not more democracy," Dieu says. "But to have more food and clothes, one must have more democracy. Without a democratic system, you have a dictatorship, social diseases in society can't be avoided and the efficient development of a market economy can't be realised."

"Democracy demands pluralism, a multi-party system," the mathematician adds. "Democracy means everyone must have the right to express what he thinks. In a democracy, you must have different political forces and organisations guaranteeing the rights of the people."

Some intellectuals who have made similar demands, such as the writer Duong Thu Huong and the physician Nguyen Dan Que, have ended up in jail. Other professors have been squeezed out of their university jobs or had their requests to travel abroad rejected.

Dieu not only stays out of prison and retains his post as vice-chairman of Vietnam's National Centre for Scientific Research, but he continues to get permission to travel abroad, to France, the US and Japan. He is even invited to talk with Vietnamese leaders about his political views.

In September 1991, he met with newly elected party chief Do Muoi to discuss a 10-page petition Dieu had circulated prior to the party's seventh congress in June. More recently, he has participated in discussions about the crisis facing world communism at the Institute of Social Sciences, the Marxist-Leninist Institute in Hanoi and the Nguyen Ai Quoc Institute in Danang, where many of the party's leading cadres are trained.

Dieu was born in Ha Tinh, one of Vietnam's poorest provinces and the birth place of the late Ho Chi Minh. In 1954, the year Ho's troops defeated French colonial forces at Dien Bien Phu, Dieu entered Hanoi University. Eight years later, he won a scholarship to study mathematics in the former Soviet Union.

He returned to Vietnam in 1967 and began working in the Science Committee's Mathematics Institute. His wife, now retired, worked in the same institute. They have three children. The oldest daughter is studying in an economic institute in France. A second daughter is studying mathematics at Hanoi University. The third child, a son, is in the eighth grade.

Dieu was twice elected as a representative to the National Assembly between 1976 and 1981 but he says the party did not nominate him again after he made repeated calls for greater democracy.

Much of Dieu's research has focused on computer science

since he was appointed director of the Computer Science Institute in 1977. Today he is working on two major research projects: one focuses on artificial intelligence and the other on protecting information in computer databases.

But Dieu is more admired among intellectuals in Vietnam for his daring political critiques than for his scientific research. Most observers are uncertain why Dieu's pummelling of the party is tolerated, while the voices of most of the party's other strident opponents are silenced.

Some of Dieu's most cynical critics say the mathematician has been invited by the party to play the role of "token" dissident. The mathematician sharply rejects the charge. "Nobody in power has asked me to do this or that," he says. "What I do I do only [following] my conscience, my responsibility before our poor country."

Dieu believes Vietnam's party is more popular than the former Communist parties in the old Soviet Union and Eastern Europe because of its role in fighting for independence and national reunification against France and the US. "Our party had very big success . . . when it remained a party of patriotism," he says. "It got failure when it became communist."

Among the party's biggest mistakes, Dieu lists its land-reform programme in the 1950s, when thousands of landlords were killed, and its decision to shut down capitalists in the south in 1978. "We must recognise that the theories of communism and socialism have brought our country many privations: a nation divided and paralysed, a devastated economy, an impoverished and backward livelihood [and] isolation from the civilised world," he wrote in his 1991 petition to the party.

Dieu says the party's reform programme has brought a "better face" to the country's economy, but resulted in few political changes. "What I propose," he explains, "is not an end to the leadership role of the party, but an end to the dictatorship of the party. If the party gets a majority in free and democratic elections, then I will support it."

Waiting in The Ruins

Ancient capital of Hue may be restored

HUE — Vietnamese conservationists hope they will soon have the funds they need to restore the old imperial capital of Hue.

Nearly five decades of war and typhoons have ravaged the old walled citadel built on the banks of the Perfume River by Vietnam's last royal dynasty. Inside the 21-metre-thick walls of the citadel, which was surrounded by a moat, emperors of the Nguyen Dynasty constructed a Forbidden City, called the Purple City, an Imperial City, palaces, pagodas and tombs.

The city needs US$4 million to protect and restore the most important remaining royal monuments, according to Nguyen Dinh Ngo, deputy chairman of Thua Thien-Hue Province. Unesco launched an international appeal for Hue in 1983, but it was largely ignored because most of the non-communist world was outraged at Vietnam's 1978 invasion of neighbouring Cambodia.

Emperor Gia Long, the founder of the Nguyen Dynasty, began building the Imperial City when he moved the capital from Hanoi in the north to central Vietnam in 1802. By 1945, when King Bao Dai handed his seal to the communist revolutionaries fighting French colonial rule, the Nguyen Dynasty's 13 emperors had built more than 300 palaces, temples, mausoleums, libraries and theatres in and around the fortress of the Imperial City.

The Nguyen Dynasty used slender wooden-column supports and steep downward-sweeping roofs, abandoning their

Tomb of King Khai Dinh.

predecessors' Thang Long architectural style with its massive columns and upturned tile roofs. But the buildings still reflect the Confucian political and philosophical conception that regarded the monarch as the centre of the universe and the link between heaven and earth.

The kings and their families lived in the Forbidden Purple City, which was built inside the old Imperial City, where most offices of the central government were housed. Seven of the Nguyen kings are buried in elaborate tombs located in parks near the tree-covered hills that surround Hue. Each of the monarchs designed his own mausoleum, which includes pavilions, temples and a funeral stele detailing the reign of the king.

Only a third of these royal monuments survived the three decades of war against France and the US that began in the mid-1940s. Four of the five palaces were destroyed during three months of heavy fighting in 1947. Some buildings were levelled by French firepower, while others were burned by zealous Vietnamese revolutionaries.

"Revolutionary soldiers and ordinary people destroyed many monuments, thinking their destruction would contribute to the revolution," says Nguyen Dac Xuan, who does research on Hue's history. "People's feelings against the foreign aggressors were so high that they were ready to sacrifice everything — themselves, their children and imperial Hue."

Another 100 monuments were damaged or destroyed in 1968 when American troops fought to recapture Hue after it was overrun by communist guerillas during the Tet offensive, says Thai Cong Nguyen, director of the Hue office in charge of historic preservation.

Since the war's end in 1975, the biggest threats to the nearly 200-year-old monuments have come from the devastating typhoons that strike central Vietnam, tropical insects, thieves and neglect. A severe storm in 1985 and another in 1990 ripped off the tiled roofs of many buildings, exposing the walls and gables to water damage. Termites have attacked the ironwood framework of most of the old buildings. Thieves have drilled into the tombs of several of the former emperors in search of gold; one young man was arrested while trying to sell bronze stripped from the roof of the elaborate Southern Gate.

Nguyen, who is in charge of the historic preservation of Hue, is heartened by the 1991 Cambodian peace settlement: it means funds for preservation may follow. In recent years, he could only depend on about US$100,000 a year from the cash-strapped Vietnamese Government to try to prevent more damage to the old buildings.

In 1991, Nguyen received his first foreign funds. The Japanese Government provided US$100,000 through Unesco to restore the severely damaged roof and columns of the Southern Gate, a massive entrance to the Imperial City formerly reserved exclusively for the use of the king on festive occasions. (Everyone else, including his wives and concubines, had to enter the city through one of its three other gates.) A French film company, shooting *Indochine* in the Imperial City, also provided some funds to replace several decaying red and gold lacquered columns in the Thai Hoa (Supreme Harmony) Palace, where emperors once held national ceremonies and received foreign guests.

Hue is Vietnam's only surviving ancient capital; the four earlier capitals have all been destroyed. Nonetheless, protection of the city's monuments has suffered from the communist leadership's stress on preserving the landmarks of the country's revolutionary history and decades of propaganda that blamed the Nguyen Dynasty for "selling" Vietnam to the French in the late 19th century.

Landmarks competing with Hue on the government's priority list include the Hung Temple, dedicated to the Hung kings who founded Vietnam; Dien Bien Phu, where the communists defeated the French colonial army in 1954; the Ho Chi Minh Trail along which the North infiltrated troops and supplies in its war against the US; and Con Dao, the island where many revolutionaries were imprisoned by the French and the Americans.

But Hue's status appears to have been upgraded in the past few years, as Vietnamese historians have become more open in their assessment of the Nguyen Dynasty and begun critically evaluating the specific role of each individual king.

Xuan, for instance, brands Dong Khanh, who signed the agreement turning Vietnam over to French rule in 1884, and his two successors as henchmen of the French, but the researcher is more generous with most of the other Nguyen monarchs. "Those who say the Nguyen Dynasty gave Vietnam to foreigners don't understand our history," he says. "Most of the Nguyen kings struggled against the French."

This new perception is slowly being introduced in state-run schools. The high school history textbook for the first time credits Gia Long, the founder of the dynasty, with uniting north and south Vietnam, building the country's main north-south highway, rapidly expanding the south's agricultural land, and establishing Vietnam's first institute to train social scientists.

Singing Between The Lines

Love songs aren't just about love

HO CHI MINH CITY — *Country Band*, a fledgling music group here, has set a record of sorts for its founder, 47-year-old Tran Tien, one of Vietnam's most popular musicians.

The band has managed to survive since December 1990. That's already considerably longer than Tien's earlier music group lasted; it was shut down by the government in 1987 after only three performances.

In Ho Chi Minh City, at least, there is a growing audience for music like *Country Band*'s — mostly romantic love songs with a subtle message of protest. That's why a number of northern-born artists have migrated southwards since the end of Vietnam's war against the US in 1975.

"I came south because I thought I would be freer," Tien says. But even Ho Chi Minh City was not ready for his first group, *Black and White*, which he had put together in 1986, not long after Vietnam's Communist Party had launched reforms to move towards a market economy and grant greater freedom to artists.

Reform or no reform, however, *Black and White* quickly found itself in conflict with officialdom because of its performance of a humorous piece called "Rock About a Clock." The song's lyrics point out how the scraggly second hand of a clock works hardest, while the stubby little hour hand — which works least — gets most attention from people when they want to tell the time. "No one asks about the second hand," Tien says. "People only notice the second hand when the clock is broken."

Many people, Tien admits, interpreted the hour hand as a reference to government officials, while the second hand represented ordinary people. So after the third night of performing to enthusiastic audiences in Ho Chi Minh City, *Black and White* was banned.

"I was close to going to jail," Tien says. He rushed back to Hanoi, where he met then-party chief Nguyen Van Linh, who protected him. Nevertheless, "I was also barred from writing new songs and performing — not by an official order like the one that disbanded my rock group, but by quiet words in my ears," Tien relates.

His comeback began with an invitation to play in the former Soviet Union in the *glasnost* heyday of late 1988. He signed a contract to play in a "Rock for Democracy" tour for six months, but he left after three months because "I was cold and missed my country." Still, Tien thinks his popularity in the Soviet Union — for decades, Hanoi's closest ally — brought him increased recognition and protection back home.

Tien first began writing songs in 1962 when he was a 17-year-old soldier in Laos fighting in the North Vietnamese army against the US-backed Vientiane regime. One time he was abandoned by his unit when he was given up as-good-as-dead from malaria. He managed to survive with help from friends. Another time he was critically wounded in the shoulder while crossing a minefield.

After this injury, Tien was released from the army and admitted to the Music Institute in Hanoi. He was graduated in 1962 with one degree in popular singing and a second in composing for symphony orchestra. After graduation, Tien began working as a journalist for Radio Hanoi, the government radio station, but he was not allowed to perform his songs in public.

"Hanoi at that time hated popular music," he says. "It was state policy." When his music was banned officially in 1979, Tien decided to move south.

Unlike most popular singers in Vietnam, who favour blue jeans and T-shirts, Tien often wears the olive green uniform of the Vietnamese army during his performances. Many of his songs depict the suffering of soldiers and raise questions about the results of Vietnam's "liberation wars" against France and the US.

"Footprint of a Crutch on the Beach" describes an ocean wave washing away the small round holes left in the sand by a wounded soldier's crutch. "I wanted to remind people that everything the soldiers gave [the country] during the war has come to nothing — like a footprint on the beach," he explains.

"Goodbye, Swift Bird" describes the deep disappointment of a soldier who returns home at the end of the war only to find his girlfriend has left "like a bird which sings about the spring." Tien's fans say this song reflects the disappointment of many war veterans, who feel that the Communist Party has forgotten many of the ideals for which they had struggled for decades.

Although Tien sings about the futility of war, he denies that he is against war as such. "In reality, war has to take place, but people hate war," he says. "It is the artist's duty to talk about peace, charity and humanity . . . The Vietnamese are always proud of their victory over the US, but they have forgotten to provide necessities for ordinary life, such as rice, water — and roses."

Down the Tubes

Will new money destroy quaint old buildings?

HANOI — The heart of this ancient city is a network of small, tree-lined streets and low, narrow houses with curved, red-tiled roofs. The downtown shophouses have long captured the imagination of Vietnamese artists and foreign visitors. But Hanoi's old commercial quarter is now threatened with extinction.

Already ravaged by decades of neglect and overcrowding, the area is now falling victim to the city's new moneyed elite. Merchants who have accumulated capital under the Communist Party's recent economic reforms are replacing the old houses with the same type of tall, flat-roofed shophouses with grate-metal doors that have become so popular in other Asian capitals.

City officials bemoan the rapid destruction of Hanoi's unique architectural heritage and recognise that this could rob the Vietnamese capital of its main attraction for tourist dollars. But they have failed so far to introduce stiff laws to halt the trend.

"If the People's Committee doesn't adopt regulations soon to protect Hanoi's architecture, then in two, three or five years there will be nothing left to protect," says Nguyen Truc Luyen, head of the capital's Union of Architects. Luyen estimates that half of the old houses already have been destroyed, but most observers believe the actual figure is much higher.

The so-called "36 Streets" area, lying in the heart of Hanoi around Hoan Kiem (or "returned sword") Lake, has its origins in the 11th century, when King Ly Thai To shifted the Vietnamese capital to Hanoi. In the centuries that followed, craftsmen and merchants moved in from the countryside and set up guilds to provide handicrafts and consumer goods for the royal family and its staff, who lived in a nearby citadel.

Different types of craftsmen — silversmiths, leather workers, dyers and so on — settled together according to their trades, giving names to the "36 Streets" by which they are still known today. The area continued to prosper despite later changes: the shift of the capital to Hue, in central Vietnam, 800 years later and the French colonisation of the country in the late 19th century.

As the "36th Streets" became more densely populated, the residents developed a unique architectural style — long, narrow dwellings known as "tube houses," designed to give each family a room fronting onto the street from which to do business. Many of the surviving tube houses, built in the late 19th and early 20th centuries, are as little as two metres wide but can be up to 60-100 metres long.

The front room of a typical tube house can be opened up by removing sliding wooden panels from a large window to turn it into a shop for selling the household's products. Behind the shop is an open-air inner courtyard, which provides light, ventilation, and a place for relaxing and raising decorative fish or ornamental plants. Next come the family's living quarters, followed by another courtyard that includes the kitchen and bathroom.

The most charming feature of these old tube houses are the low, upturned roofs covered with homemade red tiles. The walls are made of bricks held together with a mixture

Hanoi tube house

185

of sugar-cane juice, sand and lime; Vietnam did not have cement when the houses were built.

Although the "36 Streets" escaped US bombing in the 1960s and early 1970s, the old houses began deteriorating rapidly during the war years due to lack of maintenance, as all resources and energy were devoted to defeating the Americans. Without repair, many of the roofs began to leak, which caused their wood supports to rot and the masonry walls to become unstable.

The decline continued after the end of the war because the victorious communist government ploughed most of its resources into building new factories and upgrading its army. Tube house tenants felt uncertain about whether the state would allow them to continue living where they were, so they invested little of their own capital in fixing up the premises.

Hanoi's exploding post-war population — it has nearly quadrupled to over 3 million since 1954 — puts further pressure on the old houses. Today five, seven and even 10 extended families occupy some of these traditional dwellings, which were designed originally to house only one family. The average resident of the "36 Streets" has only 1.5 square metres of living space, less than half the already meagre 3.6 square metres per person in other parts of Hanoi, according to architect Luyen.

The overcrowding and the deteriorating condition of the old houses have prompted many of the area's merchant families to upgrade and expand their houses, now that they once again have begun accumulating money thanks to the economic reforms introduced in 1986. But, because of land scarcity in the area, most new construction is upwards, which violates the traditional skyline of the "36 Streets."

The result is a spate of new flat-roofed, three- or four-storey structures of the sort that already mar the commercial areas of other Asian cities. In theory, Hanoi prohibits this architectural style in the "36 Streets" area, "but these [regulations] exist mainly on paper," admits Trinh Hong Trieu, deputy director of the city's Construction Department. "Often when people apply for a building licence, they have already built the house according to their wishes. After they're caught, they have to pay a fine, but it's so low that they're willing to pay it."

Trieu says the city is currently drafting stiffer laws. But the cash-strapped Hanoi government has plenty of other pressing problems on its mind, such as controlling the serious flooding in the city.

Lest architectural conservation gets lost in the shuffle, Luyen and others urge local officials to concentrate on only a small area for protection. They also recommend that the new laws should insist only on preserving the traditional roofs and facades of the tube houses, allowing tenants to upgrade the areas away from the street.

But Trieu admits that even these modest regulations could prove unpopular with residents in the "36 Streets." "The majority of citizens there want modern houses, so it's difficult to struggle against them," he says. To tackle this problem, Hoang Huu Phe, a Vietnamese architect studying at the Asian Institute of Technology in Bangkok, has suggested that Hanoi introduce incentives, such as business tax reductions, for households financing their own repairs of the traditional houses.

A report on the area prepared for Unesco in 1990 recommended that the city find ways to relocate some of the area's dense population, but officials say this will be almost impossible because of the lucrative location of the old quarter. "People don't want to move," says Luyen. "They are used to life here and they use their houses not only for living but for making their livelihood."

But many Vietnamese and foreign residents of Hanoi are worried that the continuing debate over regulations is dragging on too long. "If they don't do something fast, they'll spoil the town," warns a cultural attache at a Western embassy. "If Hanoi wants to develop tourism, they'll have to preserve the 36 Streets. If they turn Hanoi into a new Bangkok, no one will come."

Is the Party Over?

It could survive by being less communist

HANOI — Will the Vietnamese Communist Party be able to withstand the political earthquakes that have swept from power its long-standing allies in the former Soviet Union and Eastern Europe?

"I see a chance for the party to survive — if it renovates its ideology, increases internal party democracy and separates itself from the daily running of the government," argues a Vietnamese intellectual, reflecting the views of many Vietnamese and foreign observers.

"But communism won't survive. It has no reality in Vietnam," he says. "Every time the party tries to realise communist ideals it faces disaster."

Near-economic collapse and international isolation had forced Vietnam's communists by 1986 to abandon old-time Marxist-Leninist orthodoxy and adopt free-market economics. But most analysts doubt that the changes in the former Soviet bloc will lead to a popular uprising that will force the Vietnamese party to accept a liberal democracy, at least in the next few years.

"It's impossible for the Vietnamese to depose their leading figures like the Romanians ousted [Nicolae] Ceausescu," a diplomat argues, alluding to the violent overthrow of the former East European party chief. "The party's mistakes after 1975 weren't as bad as in some other communist countries." He suggests that Hanoi's human-rights record was better than that of many other communist parties despite its brutal land-reform programme in 1956 and the harsh re-education camps

Nguyen Van Linh, architect of 1986 reform plan.

it established after 1975.

"Vietnamese communists always understood how to keep four-fifths of the population in the countryside quiet," he says. "I see the changes in Vietnam as evolutionary, rather than revolutionary."

One reason for this view lies in the popular perception of the Vietnamese party. In Eastern Europe, many resented the imposition of communist rule by an outside power — the Soviet Union. In Vietnam, the party has deep local roots and even the most vehement anti-communists believe it played a key role in gaining the country's independence from France and the US.

In addition, the Vietnamese party defused much popular discontent by admitting its mistakes and beginning economic reforms in the mid-1980s, rather than waiting until domestic discontent had exploded. "The party realised early it had to reform or else it would collapse," one official observes.

The party's decision to abandon unpopular farm cooperatives and allow the return of private enterprise has brought improved living conditions for many people. Although the party has tolerated only cautious political liberalisation, it has eased its earlier Stalinist controls on artists, intellectuals and journalists, granted greater freedom to religious believers, ended its repression of the ethnic Chinese minority and freed many of its political prisoners.

Despite the Vietnamese party's apparent assets, the collapse of socialism in Eastern Europe and the Soviet Union sent shockwaves through Vietnam's leadership. Not only had Moscow long served as Hanoi's political patron, but the former Soviet Union also had bankrolled the Vietnamese government, offered it security guarantees through its Treaty of Friendship and trained many of its bureaucrats and technicians.

When the ruling Central Committee met in August 1989 as the communist parties in Eastern Europe began collapsing, the Vietnamese leadership declared its rejection of political pluralism in Vietnam and accused Western countries, especially the US, of trying to undermine world socialism.

Nguyen Van Linh, party chief at the time and architect of Vietnam's 1986 reform programme, declared that the party had reached a "very high level of unanimity" in rejecting calls for "bourgeois liberalisation, pluralism, political plurality and multi-opposition parties aimed at denying Marxism-Leninism." In another speech to the plenum, Linh insisted that "democracy, either real or formal, does not depend on one or many parties."

"Democratisation is now essentially directed at the economic domain," Linh said in a National Day speech a week later. "It is not our policy to hasten renovation of the political system while preparations are still inadequate. Neither is it our intention to effect limitless democratisation," he said. "Any adventurous step in this direction would certainly lead to political instability."

Since then, Vietnamese officials have regularly repeated the theme that a multi-party democracy would bring political chaos, derailing the country's recent limited economic success. "I think in the near future a multi-party regime would not help Vietnam," argues Tran Bach Dang, who served as party chief in Saigon during the war with the US. "Strict democracy only brings disorder," he says, alluding to the chaos in the former Soviet Union.

"If a multi-party system is necessary, we won't be able to avoid it," says Dang, now an intellectual and frequent government critic. "But if it's not a necessity and we introduce this system, it could ruin our economic development."

The Vietnamese party had begun reining in political reform in early 1989, even before the turmoil erupted in Eastern Europe. In a speech that February, Linh had warned the press against publishing reports that undermined public confidence in the party and told journalists that they remained "tools" of the party. In the months that followed, the director of the Central Committee's Department of Culture and Ideology and several outspoken newspaper editors were fired and some literary magazines were shut down.

At the same time, the Ministry of Interior's security apparatus, which monitors dissident activities, was boosted to 180,000 personnel from about 150,000 and an elite unit of the army was trained to suppress any potential internal uprisings.

At the next Central Committee plenum in March 1990, the party sacked its leading advocate of political reform, Tran Xuan Bach, who ranked ninth in the Politburo. Bach had been increasingly outspoken prior to the meeting, arguing that the party needed to introduce broader political reforms. "One cannot think that turbulence will occur only in Europe," he warned. "There is still unrest among the people. They are demanding more democracy and social justice."

Despite the party's warning shots, other prominent dissidents continued criticising the country's communist rulers. Shortly before the seventh party congress in June 1991, Nguyen Khac Vien, then a 78-year-old intellectual who had long served as a propagandist for the party, issued a petition calling for the resignation of the country's leaders and the introduction of wide-ranging democratic freedoms.

The party's leadership is "totally impotent," the French-trained paediatrician warned, "plunging the country into disorder and preventing all development." Politburo members "do not understand that many comrades are too old, physically inept, and incapable of following the changing times," he charged. "Unless a set of broad-based rules for democracy are drawn up and implemented, the country will never be able to stand alone and compete with its neighbouring countries."

Similar criticisms were levelled by other widely respected intellectuals, including mathematician Phan Dinh Dieu, economist Hong Ha and writer Duong Thu Huong, who was arrested shortly before the congress. Although the party faces no organised domestic opposition, party leaders seem to fear that their critics enjoy considerable quiet support.

"It is regrettable that even from the ranks of communists, there have been manifestations of indecision in terms of political stance, and trends negating the achievement of socialism, leading to the negating of the socialist path altogether," outgoing party chief Linh told the June 1991 congress.

Although most analysts believe the party faces no immediate threat to its monopoly hold on power, many suggest it is entering a period of deep political crisis. One problem is that the economic reforms are gradually eroding the party's power. By abandoning farm cooperatives, encouraging private enterprise and relaxing its restrictions on artists and writers, the party has weakened its grip over Vietnamese society.

"Ordinary people have rejected the party's dogma," one official observes. "Nowadays they're going their own way, ignoring the party."

As the party has dropped its rigid social controls, greed, corruption, smuggling, drug addiction and prostitution have veered out of control. Although Vietnam now is a gentler country in which to live, the government appears to lack the will and the technocrats with skills to introduce new laws to govern the economy, social order, and even traffic in the cities. People seem free to do almost anything as long as they do not challenge the communists' hold on power.

The party is suffering further from an "ideological vacuum," following the collapse of its long-time mentor party in the former Soviet Union. "The party follows old Marxist-Leninist concepts about class struggle and exploitation which date back to the end of the 19th century," observes one official. "This dogmatic and outdated thinking causes serious incompetence among party leaders. How can the party play a leading role in the country without a clear conception" of its goals?

At the same time, the party's collective leadership style often paralyses political decision making, while the different political and geographical factions in the ruling 13-man Politburo struggle to find a compromise. In recent years, the need for consensus has prompted endless wrangling over problems such as whether and how to privatise money-losing state enterprises that are draining the government's limited resources.

The economic reforms also have exacerbated tensions between Hanoi and local party bosses. This problem dates back to the wars against France and the US, when provincial leaders ran little independent fiefdoms. Now the reforms are once again fuelling decentralisation and local independence.

In addition, economic liberalisation is compounding the gulf between the south and north. The southern provinces have benefited most quickly from the reforms, thanks to surging rice production in the Mekong delta and Ho Chi Minh City's ability to capture more than 40% of the capital pledged by foreign investors. This success has prompted growing impatience in the south for more rapid reform and greater autonomy.

Party control in the south is shorter-lived and still weaker than in north. Only 1% of the population in the south has joined the party, compared with 9% in the north and 16% in Nghe Tinh, the northern coastal province where former president Ho Chi Minh was born. Nationwide, the party in 1991 had some 2 million members, or roughly 3% of the population.

Another problem is the declining ethical standards among party members. A 1989 party study found that less than one-third of its members still maintained their "revolutionary" qualities.

"The party faces serious ideological erosion," one official complains. "The police are drunk, party bosses in the countryside are trying to accumulate land and the sons of the bosses are running private companies. The party has lost its heroic past."

Coupled with this, the party is having increasing difficulties recruiting new members. In 1987, it recruited 100,000 new members, but in 1989 this figure fell to 66,000 and in 1991 only 36,000 people signed up. A May 1992 article in *Nhan Dan*, the party daily, said fewer soldiers, intellectuals and students want to join the party because of the collapse of communism in the former Soviet bloc and the country's economic problems.

To make matters worse, the party is losing some of its old members. In early 1992, the party daily reported that 7,000 members had been expelled in Hai Hung province, east of Hanoi, in a "rectification campaign." In one district of the province, 21 members had quit in 1990 and another 200 dropped out in 1991. "Some of them occupied high positions at the provincial level and others had been party members for 40 years," the paper said.

The party also claims that "imperialist plots" are trying to destroy communist rule in Vietnam. In a September 1992 speech to his troops, Defence Minister Doan Khue warned that hostile forces were trying to overthrow the party using military means and "peaceful evolution," a term also used by China to describe efforts by Western countries to introduce ideas advocating political pluralism. Khue said unidentified enemies were taking advantage of "our mistakes in order to maliciously arouse and spread doubt and vagueness."

Officials say anti-communist overseas Vietnamese groups, with strong support in the US, France and other Western countries, have stepped up their activities against Hanoi. "After the former Soviet Union collapsed, they imagined that their time had come so they are trying to make noisier activities in Vietnam," says Ha Xuan Truong, the former editor of *Communist Review*.

Some Vietnamese analysts believe the internal challenges facing the party eventually will bring it down. "The party is now in self-destruction process," says a technocrat in Hanoi. "Neither 20 years of anti-communist propaganda nor CIA activities have succeeded in doing what the party is doing to itself," he says, alluding to such problems as growing corruption and internal political bickering.

But most Vietnamese and foreign analysts still doubt that the party will collapse or be toppled from power any time soon, despite the challenges it faces. They cite the apparent ability of senior leaders to remain united and continue to impose their will on the country.

In addition, the country lacks a well-organised opposition movement calling for a multi-party political system. "The suppression is too high, and people prefer to earn money, rather than get involved in politics," an intellectual says.

Nevertheless, many Vietnamese believe the party will be forced to take further steps away from old-style communism as it embraces free-market economics and seeks to integrate the country into Southeast Asia. But few Vietnamese observers, including the party's harshest critics, believe the country will soon have a pluralistic political regime. Some, however, are convinced that 10 years from now, Vietnam's party will look strikingly similar to the non-communist ruling parties in nearby Singapore and Indonesia, which hold a tight monopoly on political life in those countries.

ALL-ASIA
TRAVEL
GUIDE

If You Go . . .

✈ Entry

A sharp rise in the number of businessmen and tourists visiting Vietnam has put flights under considerable pressure — particularly flights out of Ho Chi Minh City, which each year serve tens of thousands of visiting overseas Vietnamese and Vietnamese emigrating to the West.

A dramatic surge in the number of flights since 1990 has helped ease the pressure. But steadily rising demand, combined with Vietnam's haphazard booking system, means travellers should reconfirm their reservations for their outward journey on arrival. Even then there can be problems with queue-jumpers paying under the counter for their seats.

Bangkok, long the main point of departure for Vietnam, now faces increasing competition from Hongkong, Singapore, Kuala Lumpur and Taipei. Thai International operates three flights weekly between Bangkok and Hanoi, while Vietnam Airlines operates seven. Thai flies from Bangkok to Ho Chi Minh City five time a week and Hanoi nine times. Three Air France flights from Paris to Ho Chi Minh City and one from Paris to Hanoi also stop in Bangkok.

Cathay Pacific and Vietnam Airlines jointly operate daily flights between Hongkong and Ho Chi Minh City and fly between the British colony and Hanoi three times each week. Singapore Airlines and its Vietnamese counterpart provide joint daily service between Singapore and Ho Chi Minh City and link the Vietnamese capital to Singapore three times a week. Two Lufthansa flights from Frankfurt to Ho Chi Minh

City stop in Singapore.

China Airlines and Eva Air of Taiwan have five flights each week between Taipei and Ho Chi Minh City, while Vietnam's Pacific Airlines flies the route four times. Either Malaysian Airlines or Vietnam Airlines provide daily service from Ho Chi Minh City to Kuala Lumpur, while Malaysian has a direct flight from the Malaysian capital to Hanoi every Monday. Three flights a week link Manila to Ho Chi Minh City.

Cambodian Airlines and Vietnam Airlines operate nine flights each week between Phnom Penh and Ho Chi Minh City, but only one from the Cambodian capital to Hanoi. Lao Aviation and Vietnam Airlines link Hanoi and Vientiane three times a week, while linking Ho Chi Minh City to the Lao capital two times.

China Southern Airlines in 1992 began a twice-weekly service between Canton and Ho Chi Minh City and once-weekly Hanoi-Peking flights. Aeroflot flies between Hanoi and Moscow twice a week. Four or five flights operate daily between Hanoi and Ho Chi Minh City.

Immigration

All visitors need visas. Businessmen require sponsorship by a government agency or a company that acts as the visitor's host. Tourists should apply through a travel agent whether they intend to travel independently or with a tour group. Embassies require applications at least a week in advance of one's departure date, while travel agencies often need at least three weeks.

Vietnamese missions in Western capitals include Bonn, London, Ottawa, Paris, Rome and Stockholm. Other major embassies are located in Bangkok, Canberra, Jakarta, Kuala Lumpur, Manila, Tokyo and Vientiane. Hongkong has a consulate and Taipei has a trade office that issue visas. Travel agencies in Bangkok, Hongkong, Taipei and Singapore offer tours to Ho Chi Minh City only, or longer trips including visits to Hanoi, Hue and Danang.

Within 48 hours of arrival, all foreign visitors must regis-

197

ter with the police. In Hanoi, contact the Immigration Office (89 Tran Hung Dao) and in Ho Chi Minh City go to the Foreigners' Service of the City Public Security Dept (161 Nguyen Du St, Dist 1). Travel agents or your host can help with this procedure. You will need two visa photographs to complete the registration process. Visitors who do not register will be fined about US$20 when they leave.

➕ Health

Injections against cholera, hepatitis, Japanese encephalitis, tetanus and typhoid are recommended, but not required. Visitors may want to bring anti-mosquito lotion or coils and anti-diarrhoea tablets, and those travelling in highland regions should consider taking precautions against malaria. Tourists should drink only boiled or bottled water and should avoid raw vegetables. Avoid ice except in major hotels.

💲 Currency

Vietnam's currency, the dong, was valued in March 1993 at roughly Dong 10,500:US$1. There is no longer much differential between the official and free-market exchange rates. Visitors changing money on the free market should only use established shops. Avoid freelance money changers, who often cheat their customers.

The US dollar is widely required for paying hotel bills, car rental, international telephone calls, faxes, telexes and shopping. Travellers' cheques can be changed in Hanoi and Ho Chi Minh City, but only with difficulty elsewhere. **Visa** credit cards issued by non-US banks and carried by non-Americans can be used in major hotels and in some larger shops. **American Express** credit cards are not acceptable.

👄 Language

Vietnamese is the national language. A Roman script with added marks indicating tones and vowel changes is used in the written language. The spoken language differs slightly between the north, centre and south. English is spoken by many educated people. Some older people speak French, while those who studied in Moscow speak Russian.

 Climate

It is best to visit the northern part of the country between September and December, when the weather is sunny and mild. The winter from late December to February is usually chilly and cloudy. In spring, the north often suffers from almost continuous drizzly rain. Summers, especially June to August, can be unpleasantly hot and humid.

Conditions in the southern part of Vietnam are warm to hot throughout the year with the average daily maximum exceeding 31°C. At night temperatures drop to around 23°C. April and May are the hottest months, when temperatures often reach 35°C and the humidity is very high. The most pleasant months in the south are November to January. The rainy season in Ho Chi Minh City lasts from about June to September. The rainy season around Danang and Hue in the centre is from about October to March.

Temperatures in the northern or central highlands are much lower than those in coastal areas. The average annual temperature in Dalat is 19.4°C.

Dress

Lightweight clothing is sufficient in Ho Chi Minh City all year round. Heavy sweaters and wind-resistant jackets are needed in the North during the winter months, when temperatures often drop to 8°C or lower. Warmer clothing is also needed in the highlands, especially at night.

Business Hours

Working hours for government offices are from about 7:30-11:30 a.m. and 1-4:30 p.m. from Monday to Saturday. Banks are open from 7:30-11:30 a.m. and 1-3:30 p.m. Monday to Friday. Banks are also open on Saturday mornings. Private shops and restaurants open around 8:30 a.m. and close rather late in the evening. They are usually open seven days a week.

🤝 Doing Business

Few Vietnamese officials or businessmen speak English, but most of them have translators. It is important to ascertain politely but quickly how well the translator speaks English, because many of them pretend they understand even when they do not.

A visitor should carry plenty of business cards, because the Vietnamese are almost as fond of exchanging them as are the Japanese. Vietnamese men normally shake hands when greeting foreign visitors, but women traditionally do not shake hands with each other or with men. A visitor should only shake hands with a woman if she extends her hand first.

Vietnamese social relations are governed by politeness and modesty. The Vietnamese way is to talk around a sensitive point, assuming the listener will infer the meaning. Stressing the importance of harmonious relations, Vietnamese generally avoid direct confrontation. Westerners commonly associate a smile with pleasure and amusement, but in Vietnam it can also symbolise embarrassment, anxiety, frustration and anger.

Most Vietnamese officials and businessmen are punctual, but they often frustrate foreigners by appearing not to feel a lot of pressure to accomplish things quickly. A foreign businessman needs to make certain that the person he is talking to is in fact in a position to make a decision. Some of the most successful foreign firms in Vietnam are those that have found dynamic counterparts.

Touching someone on the head or pointing the sole of one's foot at another person is considered rude. It is also impolite to hail another person by waving a finger or hand in the upright position. Instead, Vietnamese summon each other by waving their hands in a cupped, downward position indicating "come to my side, sit with me." Nonetheless, the Vietnamese are hospitable people. As long as a visitor remains polite and calm, it is unlikely that he will seriously offend his hosts.

Business visitors will find that their business or government counterparts wear shirts and ties in Ho Chi Minh City and in Hanoi during the hot summer months. Suits are commonly worn for official functions and in Hanoi during the autumn, winter and spring. Vietnamese women, who play a significant role in business and government circles, commonly wear dress trousers or skirts and blouses.

Vietnamese businessmen often entertain their guests in restaurants. Most Vietnamese men love to drink beer and smoke cigarettes while partying. Vietnamese commonly toast each other with "*chuc suc khoe*," which translates as "wish you health." Vietnamese women rarely smoke or drink, at least in public.

Vietnamese usually begin a friendly conversation by asking about their guest's wife and children. They are open to discussing almost any subject, but a visitor should be cautious about raising overtly political questions until being well acquainted with his host.

A visitor wanting to give a gift to a Vietnamese male counterpart would rarely go wrong if he gave a carton of 555 or Marlboro cigarettes or a bottle of Johnnie Walker whisky.

Car rentals along with translation and secretarial services are available in many of the major hotels such as the Pullman Metropole in Hanoi and the Floating, Century Saigon, Continental and Rex in Ho Chi Minh City.

🖐️ Rip-Offs

As in many other Asian countries, a visitor needs to bargain for almost everything, including taxis, food in markets, handicrafts and art works. One should beware of fakes. The Vietnamese are masterful at faking antiques and art pieces as well as brand name alcohol and medicine.

Many shopkeepers also try to cheat their customers by giving short measure of almost anything being weighed.

One should only change money in banks or established shops. "Freelance bankers" on the street offer higher rates, but commonly swindle their customers.

Those walking the streets of Ho Chi Minh City should beware of young boys selling maps and post cards, heavily made-up transvestites and beggars, any of whom may be masterful at picking pockets for wallets and stealing watches, necklaces, pens or even glasses.

 ## Media

A growing number of newspapers and magazines are being published in English. The Vietnam News Agency publishes the daily *Vietnam News* and a daily bulletin. The Ho Chi Minh People's Committee publishes a weekly called *Saigon Times* and the Institute for Research on Market and Price in Hanoi puts out the weekly *Market & Price* bulletin, which gives weekly price information. Vietnam *Investment Review*, published by a joint venture between Vietnam's State Committee for Investment and Cooperation and an Australian firm, provides business and investment news.

Magazines such as the *Far Eastern Economic Review*, *Time* and *Newsweek*, along with English-language dailies from Thailand, can be bought in many of the major hotels. Young boys also hustle foreign-language publications around the main hotels in Ho Chi Minh City.

☎ Communications

International direct-dial telephone services, fax and telex services are now available in most hotels in the major cities, but a visitor may have difficulty contacting the outside world from remote provinces. International calls cost at least twice as much as in neighbouring countries. Many business centres charge by the page for faxes, rather than by the length of the call. A mobile phone service has been introduced in Ho Chi Minh City.

🚗 Transport

Taxis are available at the Hanoi and Ho Chi Minh City airports, but the fare into the city (about US$25 and US$10, respectively) should be agreed in advance. For transport around Hanoi, cars with drivers can be rented from **Fuji Cab** (Tel: 252-452), **Mansfield Toserco** (Tel: 269-444) and **Car Rental Service** No. 12 (Tel: 254-074) and many hotels.

In Ho Chi Minh City, a new fleet of taxis began plying the streets in late 1992 in search of customers. Cars and drivers can be rented from **Saigon Tourist Car Rental Co.** (Tel: 295-925), **Saigon Auto Salon** (Tel: 291-505), **Fidi Tourist** (Tel: 296-264) and most major hotels.

In all cities and towns, visitors can hire cyclos — three-wheeled pedicabs — for a modest fare, but they must be sure that the driver understands the destination.

The one-way air fare for foreigners between Hanoi and Ho Chi Minh City is US$150. Travel by train is now open to visitors and is cheaper than flying. But trains are often congested, the comforts minimal and the journey times quite variable. Buses also operate between major cities, but they are even more rugged.

Accommodation

Hotel reservations can be made directly but it is most reliable for visitors to contact the travel agencies or individuals hosting their trip. The increasing number of visitors has put pressure on existing hotels, making it harder to find rooms and causing prices to rise. An increasing number of small guesthouses have begun operating in major cities.

In Hanoi, the **Pullman Metropole** is the only four-star hotel, with rooms beginning at US$129. The **Thang Loi**, located on beautiful West Lake, is rather remote, but has rooms for US$52, while the new **Saigon Hotel** has rooms beginning at US$50. The centrally located **Government, Military and Energy** guesthouses offer accommodation from US$27-55. Visitors can also stay at the somewhat rundown old French hotels such as the **Dan Chu**, **Hoa Binh** and **Hoan Kiem**.

Ho Chi Minh City has two luxury hotels: the **Saigon Floating** and the **Century Saigon**, offering rooms beginning at US$175 and US$95, respectively. The comfortable **Continental** and **Rex** also have business centres and provide rooms from about US$60. Newly opened joint-venture hotels include the **Norfolk** and **Saigon Star**, which have rooms from around US$60-70. Other popular, but slightly rundown hotels include the **Caravelle**, **Mondial**, **Majestic** and **Friend-ship**, with rooms starting at US$35-50.

Major tourist spots at **Ha Long Bay** and **Do Son** sea resort in the north; **Hue**, **Danang**, **Nhatrang** and **Dalat** in the centre; **Vung Tau**, **Can Tho**, **My Tho** and **Ben Tre** in the south also have hotels, but the accommodation is often rather spartan.

🍽 Dining

Many Vietnamese restaurants are small, insignificant spots that serve delightful specialities, but visitors often have trouble making themselves understood and may be put off by the modest hygiene. However, the recent economic liberalisation has spawned a dramatic increase in the number of restaurants, some of which are of excellent quality.

Vietnamese cooking, comparable to Chinese but often more spicy, offers considerable variety. The best-known seasoning is *nuoc mam*, Vietnamese fish sauce. Herbs and spices such as coriander, lemon grass, mint, pepper and a local variety of basil provide a light, subtle flavour. Many cooks use liberal quantities of monosodium glutamate in their cooking.

The long coastline means that excellent seafood is available. The French influence is apparent in the availability of excellent *baguettes*. Many visitors are attracted to *cha gio* or *nem Saigon*, deep fried spring rolls with pork or crab meat, egg, vermicelli and chopped vegetables. *Bo bay mon*, beef served seven ways, is popular, with each dish accompanied by its own traditional sauce and vegetables. *Cha tom* is ground seasoned shrimp grilled on sugarcane skewers, which add a sweetness to the shrimp. *Banh hoi* is a thin noodle eaten with barbecued pork balls, fish sauce and fresh vegetables.

The southern *canh chua*, sour fish soup with pineapple and bean sprouts, is also tasty. *Pho*, the popular noodle soup, comes in many varieties, depending on the meat, noodles and other ingredients used.

All the hotels in Hanoi and Ho Chi Minh City serve some sort of Western food, but they are facing increasing competition from the burgeoning number of private restaurants. The only first-class restaurant in the capital is that in the **Pullman Metropole** hotel.

Other popular restaurants serving a variety of Western and Vietnamese cuisine include **202** (at 202 Hue St), **Lotus** (16 Ngo Quyen), **Piano Bar** (50 Hang Vai St), **Piano Bar and Restaurant** (93 Phung Hung), **Rose** (15 Tran Quoc Toan St) and **Bistrot** (34 Tran Hung Dao St). **La Vong** (14 Cha Ca St) has refined its popular fish speciality over five generations.

Restaurants in Ho Chi Minh City offer greater variety and better service. Centrally located restaurants providing excellent Vietnamese cuisine include **Thanh Nien** (135 Hai Bai Trung St), which also has the city's best Italian ice cream and "piano bar," **Vietnam House** (93-95 Dong Khoi St, Dist 1) and **VY** (105 Yersin St).

Madam Dai's (84A Nguyen Du, Dist 1), located in the library of the French-trained lawyer, Nguyen Phuoc Dai, serves both Vietnamese and French food, but advance reservations are a must. **Le Mekong** (159 Ky Con, Dist 1) offers delightful French fare, while **Chez Guido** located in the Continental Hotel, has the only broad selection of pasta and pizza in Vietnam.

Japanese food is served at the **Nihon Basi** (Rex Hotel) and **Kiku** (Caravelle Hotel). Korean food is available at **Seoul House** (37 Ngo Duc Ke St, Dist 1) and **Angel** (34 Le Duan St, Dist 1).

Favourite bars for foreign businessmen include **Tiger Tavern** (225 Dong Khoi St, Dist 1) and **City Bar & Grill** (63 Dong Khoi St, Dist 1). **Apocalypse Now** and **B-4-75** (as in "Before 1975," the year the Vietnam War ended and Vietnam was reunified under communism), on Dong Du St in Dist 1, are popular with younger tourists and American war veterans because of their war memorabilia and ear-splitting music from the late 1960s and early 1970s.

🎵🍸 Entertainment

Ho Chi Minh City remains the entertainment capital of Vietnam, boasting a variety of discos and dancing establishments. Massage parlours and more risque bars known as *bia om* (literally "hugging bars") have reopened in recent years, although they are occasionally shut down for brief periods by the police.

Among the most fashionable dancing establishments are the **Super Star** (201/3 Hoang Viet St, Tan Binh Dist) and **Arc-en-ciel** (52-56 Tan Da St, Dist 5) as well as the discos in hotels such as the **Floating, Century Saigon, Rex, Friendship** and **Caravelle**. **Maxim's**, next to the Caravelle, offers a band and singing along with food of rather modest quality. Karaoke bars have also sprouted up throughout the city in recent years.

Hanoi, more austere and without Ho Chi Minh City's exposure to modern Western tastes, is just beginning to develop some semblance of nightlife. Apart from the burgeoning number of small cafes, where young locals sit in near-darkness listening to Vietnamese and Western music, nightlife revolves almost entirely around a handful of dance halls, where quick steps and foxtrots are still as popular as disco dancing. Most frequented by foreign residents are the **VIP Lounge**, (62 Nguyen Du St), **Saigon Pull** (217 Doi Can St) and the **Thanh Loi Hotel** (on Saturday nights).

Every Thursday night, visitors can attend Hanoi's unique **Water Puppet Theatre**, where hidden puppetmasters immersed in a pool of water, choreograph often-hilarious scenes of peasant life.

Tourists interested in meeting Westerners living in Hanoi can stop by the German Embassy's **Bier Keller** on Wednesday nights or the Australian Embassy's **Billabong Bar** on Friday nights.

🎁 Shopping

Traditional Vietnamese handicrafts include lacquerware, carved tortoiseshell, mother-of-pearl inlaid trays and boxes, along with jewellery, ceramics, baskets, bamboo and silk products. Lacquerware is ubiquitous but the quality is often uneven.

Handmade silver bracelets, pendants and earrings make

attractive gifts and, if the silver content is not overestimated, the prices are still modest. Both Hanoi and Ho Chi Minh City have a growing number of art galleries, selling paintings at rapidly rising prices.

In Hanoi, many arts and crafts shops are located in the old quarter around **Hoan Kiem Lake**. Ho Chi Minh City's shopping area is concentrated around **Dong Khoi** and **Le Loi** streets, **Nguyen Hue Blvd** and bustling **Ben Thanh** market.

Street hawkers in Ho Chi Minh City peddle T-shirts that say "Good Morning Vietnam" and war-era Zippo lighters once popular among American GIs. They are scratched and tarnished and bear inscriptions such as "1st Cav. Div.," but it is more likely that they were recently cloned rather than left behind by American soldiers.

Some items, such as lacquerware or household goods, may be purchased in local currency but more-costly items such as art work and antiques are priced in US dollars. Visitors should bear in mind that antiques may be confiscated by customs officers if the purchaser does not have a certificate from the Ministry of Culture allowing the item to be exported.

Holidays

January 1: New Year.

January-February: Tet, or lunar New Year. The date depends on the lunar calendar and varies from year to year. A traditional family ceremony is celebrated at midnight on New Year's Eve, as the country erupts in an explosion of fireworks. Over the next few days, gifts are exchanged, well-wishing visits are made to relatives and friends, and pagodas and temples are visited. Tet is officially a three-day holiday in the cities, but at least a week in rural areas.

April 30: Reunification Day.

May 1: Labour Day.

September 2-3: National Day.

September-October: The Mid-Autumn Festival for children falls on the full-moon day of the eighth lunar month. Shops are filled with moon cakes and sell colourful lanterns.

DISCOVERING VIETNAM

HANOI

Under French rule, Hanoi became one of the most attractive cities in Asia and there is still charm in its broad, tree-lined boulevards and shady parks. Most of the visible scars of the wartime bombing have disappeared, but years of neglect and overcrowding have given Hanoi a rundown look. This is slowly being reversed by the construction boomlet that has erupted under the economic reforms launched in 1986.

Places to visit in Hanoi include **Hoan Kiem** (Returned Sword) Lake in the centre of the city, a charming lake with a small island on which stands **Turtle pagoda**. It marks the spot where, according to legend, a turtle rose from the water bearing a magic sword with which Le Loi, a 15th century Vietnamese hero, drove out the Chinese invaders.

North of the lake is the heart of ancient Hanoi, the so-called **36 Streets** area, with its low, narrow "tube houses" with curved, red-tiled roofs that have long captured the imagination of Vietnamese artists and foreign visitors. Today these houses are threatened, as merchants seek to replace them with the same kind of new shops popular in other Asian cities.

The 36 streets are still named after the craftsmen —silversmiths, leather workers and so on — who first settled in the area centuries ago. The bustling **Dong Xuan market**, built by the French but recently refurbished, is an adventure for a visitor interested in the wide variety of food and other products for sale.

South of Hoan Kiem Lake, one finds beautiful French colonial buildings dating back to the turn of the century. Among the most elegant are the **Government Guesthouse**, **State Bank**, **Metropole Hotel** and the **Opera House** and the **Catholic cathedral**.

Hundreds of people line up each day outside the Russian-built, marble **Ho Chi Minh Mausoleum**, waiting for an opportunity to pay homage to the first president of independent, communist Vietnam. Nearby the Russians also built a museum that exhibits the still-venerated leader's personal belongings, including his famous sandals cut from a rubber tyre. Visitors are also welcome to visit the simple two-storey wooden house on stilts where Ho lived.

The **Chua Mot Cot** (or One-Pillar Pagoda), which many people believe looks like Buddha sitting on a lotus flower, was first built in the 11th century to honour Buddhist advisers who supported Ly Thai To, the founder of ancient Hanoi. Another popular Hanoi site is the **Dong Temple**, built by Ly in memory of a mythical three-year-old hero who brandished a sword and rode an iron horse to repel a Chinese invasion around 1,000 BC.

Visitors interested in the arts can visit the **Fine Arts Museum**, located near **Van Mieu** or "Temple of Literature," Hanoi's first university built in the 11th century to honour Confucius. Many of the country's early scholars passed examinations here and their achievements are recorded on stone stele.

Of interest are tours of the **History Museum**, including its bronze drums dating back some 3,000 years, and the **Revolutionary** and **War** museums, depicting Vietnam's almost continuous struggles against China, France, Japan and the US. Interested tourists can also visit the colourful flower villages on the north side of **West Lake**.

UPCOUNTRY

Special permits are still required to travel outside of Vietnam's major cities, but this regulation was in the process of being revised in early 1993. One of the most scenic spots in the country is **Ha Long Bay**, 164 kilometres east of Hanoi. The thousands of strangely shaped, lime rock mountains jutting out of the emerald sea resemble a Chinese silk painting. Two-thirds of the way to Ha Long lies **Haiphong**, northern Vietnam's major port. Visitors may also want to visit the popular nearby beach resort of **Do Son**.

Many Hanoi residents also frequent **Tam Dao** resort, famous for its beautiful **Thac Bac** (Silver) waterfalls, located in Vinh Phu province some 80 km north of the capital at an elevation of 1,000 metres above sea level.

On the sixth day of the first lunar month, a growing number of people attend the colourful **Co Loa Festival**, celebrating King An Duong, who in the 3rd century BC built the Co Loa citadel some 16 km northeast of Hanoi. According to a popular legend, the fortress was overrun by invading Chinese forces after the king's daughter fell in love with the invading Chinese general's son and revealed to him the fortress' defence secrets. Three remaining earthen ramparts that once protected this ancient capital have survived.

Beginning on the 15th day of the lunar New Year, tens of thousands of Vietnamese make a pilgrimage to attend the annual festival at the **Huong** (Perfume) **Pagoda**, located about 60 km south of Hanoi. The pagoda is a complex of more than 30 temples, some of them in caves and grottoes, which can be reached only by taking an hour-long sampan trip on the Yen River and then walking about two kilometres up steep mountain trails.

From the 9-11th day of the third lunar month, many Vietnamese trek to the **Hung Temple** in Vinh Phu province to attend a festival commemorating the founding of Vietnam by the Hung kings. According to a timeless legend, Vietnam originated from the union of a powerful sea god and a lovely mountain goddess. Half their 100 sons followed their father to the sea, while the other 50 went with their mother to the mountains, home of the Hung kings, who later established Vietnam.

On the 10th day of the third lunar month, visitors can also travel southeast of Hanoi to attend a festival at **Hoa Lu**, the capital established after the Chinese were defeated in AD 939. Although the Vietnamese capital was moved to present-day Hanoi in the 11th century, a citadel, two temples and the tomb of Dinh Tien Hoang, the emperor who established Hoa Lu, still survive.

Driving north or west from Hanoi to the Lao or Chinese borders, the traveller sees some of the world's most beautiful scenery — sea-blue mountain ranges, lush, green hidden valleys and craggy outcrops. The mountains around **Son La** in the west are populated by Black Tai hill tribes, while **Lao Cai** and **Lai Chau** in the far north are inhabited by Hmong minorities, who still practise slash-and-burn farming on the mountain slopes, grow opium and wear colourful traditional costumes. At **Dien Bien Phu** in the far northwest, howitzers and tanks abandoned by the French in 1954 still litter rice fields in the valley, and a visitor can tour the famous hills where French positions were overrun by Vietnamese guerillas.

Cuc Huong National Park, a wildlife preserve 200 km southwest of Hanoi, surprises its visitors with its narrow limestone canyons and the large, colourful butterflies that swarm into the area in April and May. Further south, near Vinh, once a major industrial centre levelled by US bombers during the war, is the village of **Lang Sen**, Ho Chi Minh's home village.

Continuing south is **Hue**, the former imperial capital of Vietnam's last royal dynasty. On the banks of the Perfume River, Emperor Gia Long, the founder of the Nguyen Dynasty, in 1802 began building a citadel, also known as the **Imperial City**, surrounded by 21-m thick walls and a moat. By 1945, the dynasty's 13 emperors had built more than 300 palaces, temples, mausoleums, libraries and theatres in and around the fortress of the Imperial City.

The kings and their families lived in the **Forbidden Purple City**, which was built inside the old Imperial City, where most of the offices of the central government were housed. To the south is the **Ngo Mon**, or Noon Gate, a massive entrance formerly reserved for the use of the king on festive occasions.

From the Ngo Mon, a bridge over a small moat leads to the courtyards in front of the **Thai Hoa**, or Supreme Harmony, palace. Other buildings in the Citadel include the **Dien Tho** or **Everlasting Longevity Palace**, which was built as the Queen Mother's residence, and **The Mieu** and **Hung Mieu** ceremonial buildings. Nine huge bronze **Dynastic Urns** depict the achievements of the dynasty.

Seven of the Nguyen kings are buried in elaborate tombs located in parks near the tree-covered hills that surround **Hue**. The nearest, that of **Tu Duc** (1848-83), stands in a dense pine forest on the edge of a small lake. **Khai Dinh's** (1916-1925) memorial, the most elaborate of all the tombs, is a cement palace surrounded by stone mandarins, horses and elephants.

Only a third of these royal monuments survived the three decades of war against France and the US, which began in the mid-1940s. Since the war's end in 1975, the biggest threat to the monuments has come from the devastating typhoons that strike central Vietnam, tropical insects, thieves and neglect.

Five kilometres west of Hue on the north bank of the Perfume River is the seven-storey **Phuoc Duyen Tower**, which was built in 1844 on the grounds of the **Linh Mu** (Heavenly Lady) **Pagoda**. The original pagoda has disappeared but a huge 2-tonne bell and a cylindrical stone stele remain.

Many visitors to Hue enjoy an excursion on the **Perfume River** in a small rented sampan, covered with a rounded palm roof. The town of Hue is unremarkable but it is interesting to walk around and note its more traditional atmosphere. The countryside is dotted with fascinating Buddhist temples.

From Hue, it is 112 km by road — across the spectacular **Hai Van** pass or Pass of the Clouds, which geographically divides the country into north and south — to **Danang**. This city's **My Khe beach**, dubbed **China Beach** by American soldiers in the 1960s, is one of the country's most beautiful.

Nearby is the famous **Marble Mountain**, which has a Buddhist monastery and a massive cave that is lit through a gap in the rock ceiling. Danang is also home to the **Cham Museum**, which displays some 300 stone art treasures from the Indian-influenced Champa state, which ruled the area until the 15th century.

Some 20 km south of Danang, is **Hoi An**, once the Cham

empire's busy trading port, which welcomed traders from Japan, India and China. Portuguese traders and Catholic missionaries settled here in the 17th century. Some of the original Chinese temples and the marvellous houses of wealthy merchants — with their curved ornamental tile roofs and intricate door panels — have been preserved.

HO CHI MINH CITY

Ho Chi Minh City, formerly called Saigon after the river on which it is located, is Vietnam's largest city and most dynamic business centre. Many people, even officials, still call the downtown area of the city "Saigon." In the 11th and 12th centuries, it was a seaport belonging to the Angkor kingdom, which had its capital at Angkor Wat in present-day Cambodia. Vietnamese settlers and Chinese merchants only arrived at the beginning of the 17th century, so the city lacks the ancient charm of Hanoi.

One of the city's most prominent landmarks is **City Hall**, built by the French between 1901-8 at the opposite end of bustling Nguyen Hue street from the Saigon River. The pastel yellow building with its ornate facade and elegant interior is now the headquarters for the city's People's Committee.

Other French buildings in the heart of the city's business district include the **Municipal Theatre**, which served as the National Assembly building for the US-backed South Vietnamese government until the communist victory in 1975; the **Notre Dame Cathedral**, completed in 1883; and the central **Post Office**. The **History Museum** contains artifacts illustrating the evolution of the Vietnamese culture from the Dong Son Bronze Age to current civilisation. The **Revolutionary Museum** is the former French governor's mansion that now details the wars against France and the US. Both are housed in elegant French buildings.

Gia Long's Palace, another French-era building, now contains the **American War Crimes Museum**, which displays a collection of US military equipment and has a model of the infamous "tiger cages" where many communist prisoners were held. Tourists can also visit **Reunification Hall**, which earlier served as the residence for former South Vietnamese president Nguyen Van Thieu.

Xa Loi Pagoda, a modern concrete structure and scene of agitation against the regime of former president Ngo Dinh Diem, is located about a kilometre southwest of Reunification Hall. The oldest pagoda in Ho Chi Minh City, **Giac Lam**, was completed at the end of the 17th century.

The city also has several temples honouring earlier national heroes. The **Tran Hung Dao Temple**, built in a T-shape with eight curved corners adorned with dragon and phoenix figures, commemorates Tran Hung Dao's victory over the Mongol invaders in the 13th century. The **Le Van Duyet Temple** in the suburb of **Gia Dinh** contains the tomb of the military hero who served the first Nguyen emperor.

Ho Chi Minh City's Chinatown, **Cholon**, or Big Market, dominated South Vietnam's foreign trade, rice market, foreign exchange and much of its industry during the war. The city almost ground to a halt after "socialist transformation" in 1978, but it has nearly regained its former bustle under the free-market reforms introduced in 1986.

Cholon has many good restaurants, busy markets and Chinese temples, including the 19th century **Thien Hau Temple**, dedicated to the Chinese goddess of the sea who protects sea travellers. **The An Quang Pagoda**, long known for the political activism of its monks, and the **Phu Tho Horse Race Track** are also located here.

UPCOUNTRY

Visitors interested in Vietnam's war with the US should visit the **Cu Chi Tunnel Complex**, 70 km northwest of the city. Communist guerillas hid from the Americans in an elaborate 200 km network of tunnels, including smoke-tight kitchens, a field hospital, meeting rooms and living quarters. Most of the tunnels have now collapsed, but one section has been preserved for visitors.

Two hours southeast of Ho Chi Minh City is the beach resort of **Vung Tau**, nestled between hills and the South China Sea. Vung Tau has undergone something of a facelift since it served as a rather seedy Rest and Recuperation resort for Australian soldiers during the war, but the beach is no longer as clean and its water is no longer as unpolluted as it was in the past. The city today serves as a base for foreign oil companies exploring for oil off the coast of southern Vietnam.

The vast **Mekong Delta**, a fertile area built up over the centuries with silt deposited as the nine branches of the Mekong River escape to the sea, begins south of Ho Chi Minh City. The delta is Vietnam's most important rice-producing region. Villages and individual houses lie along the irrigation and drainage canals that crisscross the region.

Visitors can easily arrange day trips to **My Tho**, some 65 km south of Ho Chi Minh City. Here they can rent a sampan for a short river cruise on one of the arms of the Mekong or cross the long ferry to **Ben Tre** and on to **Vinh Long** and **Can Tho**.

Vestiges of the ancient Oc Eo civilisation, which actively traded with India, have been discovered in the southwestern province of **Kien Giang.** Scholars have found evidence that Oc Eo was a port city belonging to Funan kingdom, which flourished from the 2nd-7th centuries and predated Angkor. Archaeologists have concluded that the city contained large temples and palaces, and its artisans were skilled in working bronze, jade, silver and gold.

Tay Ninh, 96 km northwest of Ho Chi Minh City, is the site of the **Cao Dai Temple**. The Cao Dai religion, a sect founded in the 1920s, is a synthesis of Buddhism, Confucianism, Islam and Christianity whose saints include Victor Hugo, Jesus Christ, Joan of Arc and Buddha. The elaborate temple contains pillars entwined with pink plaster dragons, and at one end is the eye of Cao Dai painted on a blue globe that represents the world.

The enchanting mountain resort of **Dalat** lies some 180 km north of Ho Chi Minh City. A visitor arriving by road from the south passes through the breathtaking **Prenn** mountain pass and by the **Da Tan La** falls.

Dalat was founded in 1893 by a French doctor, Alexander

Yersin, who recognised its therapeutic benefits. Some 1,200 m above sea level, the town overlooks **Xuan Huong** lake and is surrounded by pine tree-covered hills. The average summer temperature is 20°C, and in winter 15°C.

The city's residential area is spread out, but the centre of town is at one end of the lake. Each of the many French-style villas, with their carefully tended lawns and delightful flower gardens, look like little parks.

Dalat is on the southern edge of the central highlands, so Montagnard hilltribes people — wearing their traditional garb and carrying baskets on their backs — can be seen in the market or walking along the roads. The central highlands, until recent years populated mainly by semi-nomadic minorities such as the Rhade and Jarai, has excellent soil for growing rubber, coffee and tea. Outside of Dalat, the area's other cities — **Ban Me Thuot**, **Pleiku** and **Kontum** — have been largely off-limits to foreign visitors.

Down from Dalat to the east lies **Phan Rang**, home of the Cham, who ruled the central part of Vietnam until the end of the 15th century. Several of their brick towers, remnants of the Chams' much grander days, survive in the area. Some of the Cham surviving in the area are Hindus — eating no beef and cremating their dead — while others are Muslim — eating no pork and burying their dead.

One of the oldest Cham towers — the **Po Nagar**, built in 784 — can be found in **Nhatrang**, 100 km north of Phan Rang. Nhatrang, set against a mountain backdrop, has some of the most beautiful beaches in Vietnam. The rock islands off the coast of Nhatrang are well-known for the breeding of sea swallows. Many consider sea swallow nest soup a delicacy.

Vietnam Notebook was produced by the
Far Eastern Economic Review.
Editor: John M. Leger.
Production: Henry Chiu, Winnie Law and Leong Suk Bing.
Maps & Graphics: Ringo Chung and Ray Leung.